SOUTHERN COMFORTS

Center Books on the American South

George F. Thompson, series founder and director

SOUTHERN COMFORTS:
ROOTED IN A FLORIDA PLACE

BY SUDYE CAUTHEN

The Center for American Places
Santa Fe and Staunton

PUBLISHER'S NOTES:

Southern Comforts: Rooted in a Florida Place is the ninth volume in the *Center Books on the American South* series, George F. Thompson, series founder and director. The book was brought to publication with the generous support of the Friends of the Center for American Places, for which the publisher is most grateful. For more information about the Center for American Places and the publication of *Southern Comforts: Rooted in a Florida Place*, please see page 194.

Published 2007. First edition.
Printed in China on acid-free paper.

The Center for American Places, Inc.
P.O. Box 23225
Santa Fe, New Mexico 87502, U.S.A.
www.americanplaces.org

Distributed by the University of Georgia Press
www.ugapress.uga.edu

15 14 13 12 11 10 09 08 07   1 2 3 4 5

Southern comforts : rooted in a Florida place / by Sudye Cauthen. -- 1st ed.
       p. cm. -- (Center books on the American South)
Includes bibliographical references.
ISBN-13: 978-1-930066-58-8 (hardcover : alk. paper)
ISBN-10: 1-930066-58-9 (hardcover : alk. paper)
1. Cauthen, Sudye. 2. Cauthen, Sudye--Childhood and youth. 3. Cauthen, Sudye--Family. 4. Alachua (Fla.)--Biography. 5. Alachua (Fla.)--Social life and customs. 6. Farm life--Florida--Alachua. 7. Country life--Florida--Alachua. 8. Alachua County (Fla.)--History, Local. 9. Oxford (Miss.)--Biography. I. Title. II. Series.

 F319.A38C38 2007
 975.9'79063092--dc22
 [B]

ISBN 10 1-930066-58-9
ISBN 13 978-1-930066-58-8

Frontispiece:
Bay and Lola Collier's old cabin off Bellamy Road, 1987. Photograph © Barbara B. Gibbs. Used by permission.

for

CHARLES

REAGAN

WILSON

Tell me the landscape in which you live

and I will tell you who you are.

—Jose Ortega y Gasset

contents

list of maps

family

THIS WORK IS IN PART A RESPONSE TO THE LIFE HISTORIES OF INDIVIDUALS
WHO ENLARGED MY LIFE BY ALLOWING ME TO ENTER THEIRS. I have noted
with asterisks the names of those whose oral history transcripts, along with those
from *Alachua Portrait: The Living Heritage Project*, are available at the archives of
the Samuel Proctor Oral History Project, University of Florida, Gainesville.
Insights from my interviews with Ralph Cellon, Sr. (1903–1990), Lacy
Lancaster Doke (1892–1989), George Duke, Sr. (1903–1990), Marvin Pink
Frazier (1923–1989*), Alexander Lundy (1915–1997*), William H. Enneis
(1916–2004), and the inestimable Lucile Ellis (1908–1983) also inform these
pages. These are the voices of Alachua:

Orion Cauthen	Daddy's older brother, *b. 1902, d. 1992.*
Willie Cauthen	Daddy's younger brother, *b. 1909, d. 1980.*
Daddy	My father, Allen Goolsby Cauthen, *b. 1905, d. 1975.*
Mama	My mother, Hortense M. Cauthen, *b. 1905, d. 1991.*
Emily	My sister, *b. 1946.*
Aunt Nadine	Daddy's only sister, *b. 1913.*
Uncle Colson	Mama's only brother, *b. 1908, d. 1956.*
Aunt Nancy	Mama's only sister, *b. 1906, d. 1990.*

Chester Dampier	Machinist, farmer, *b.1898, d. 1988.*
Letha Wright DeCoursey	Sharecropper, *b. 1899, d. 1990.* *
Steve Everett	Schoolteacher, *b. 1946*
Vernon McFadden Hill	Farmer, b. 1902, *d. 1993.* *
Vada Beutke Horner	Schoolteacher, *b. 1943.*
Will Irby	Alachua native, *b. 1953.*
Jim Kelly	Horse breeder, *b. 1917, d. 1997.*
Charles Lawson	Baptist deacon, *b. 1922, d. 1989.*
Gussie Washington Lee	Church pianist, *b. 1936.*
Huldah Rivers Malphurs	Baker of bread, *b. 1908, d. 1990.* *
Tommy Malphurs	Farmer, dog breeder, *b. 1929*
Mary Lou McFadden	Farmer, *b. 1900, d. 1995.* *
Arthur Spencer, Jr.	Historian, *b. 1924*
M. N. Strickland	Mama's stepfather, *b.1883, d.1971.*
Lucile Skinner Traxler	Traxler's historian, *b. 1913, d. 1996.* *
Rebecca Wallace	Midwife, *b. 1908, d. 1990.*
Lemon Washington	Farmer, preacher, *b.1920, d.1995.* *
Emery Williams	Storyteller, *b. 1904, d. 1985.*

preface

THE OLDEST MEMORIES I CARRY ARE OF TIMES BEFORE I WAS BORN AND
OF PLACES I HAVE ENTERED BY WAY OF OTHER PEOPLE'S STORIES. In
imagination, I am fixed on a succession of earlier worlds which, if I could just get
them stitched together, would somehow make coherent to me my own existence.

The details of this story are Southern. They document my ambivalence
about my origins; that is to say, my world, a place called Alachua in north-central
Florida. More than a vehicle for understanding myself in relation to place, this
work charts the evolution of one Southern community from the late nineteenth
century into the twenty-first. It is informed not only by my own experiences and
reflections, but also by the collection of oral histories, which has been a significant
part of my life's work.

My father's death in 1975 triggered in me an impulse toward self-exami-
nation, driving me unhesitatingly from the Kennedy Space Center on the
Atlantic Coast back to the interior of the state, a rich agricultural area that once
exported cotton to the world from its antebellum plantations, a place explored
by the aboriginal Timucuans, then the Spanish, French, English, Seminoles, and
my own ancestors long before Carl Webber, in his promotional book, dubbed it in
1883 "the Eden of the South."

Not too long ago, I read Carolyn Heilbrun's proclamation that a woman's
nostalgia for childhood might mask unrecognized anger.[1] I pondered this
assertion, remembering that, during the years this book was forming inside me, I
once remarked to a friend that real estate developers were ruining Alachua. "They
are ruining my childhood," I said. "You have had your childhood," he answered,
but he was wrong. I had not and never will, except as imagination allows.

These chapters chart the subjective, emotional parallels to the objective, public work of investigating Alachua, attempts to wrest from northwestern Alachua County during the 1970s and 1980s the childhood I missed in the 1950s: I wanted to witness calves birthed and to see blood spurt at hog killings. I wanted to claim all that Daddy had protected me from, all that a Southern white girl born before the civil rights campaigns of the 1960s and the angry feminist challenges of the 1970s could not see from the top of her shaky pedestal.

Back in Alachua County, I discovered Florida's Black Hat Troubadour, Will McLean, singing "There's a wild hog/in Gulf Hammock/I don't wish/on any man."[2] I initiated the Alachua County Folk-Arts-in-the-Schools (ACFA) Program, which put McLean and other folk artists in six middle schools, where they enlivened classrooms with performances and hands-on programs in which children baked clay pots in a kiln, wrote their own songs, wove baskets of palmetto and pine needles, learned to perform the "hambone" with Bessie Jones and the Sea Island Singers, and made necklaces from bleached cow bones. Each time I read "ACFA" on one of my file folders, I was reminded of another folder so similarly identified: ACMN, "Allen Cauthen's my name," the haunting phrase Daddy used to introduce himself to the old men and women during his short stay at a nursing home.

The ACFA program, Florida's first, was launched in 1976, the year of our nation's bicentennial, in the midst of a decade of upheaval for many families in which young mothers like me, expecting the life Germaine Greer had promised, found themselves instead in long lines waiting to get certified for food stamps. In our search for freedom, which took a great deal longer than my friends and I expected, we became the "me" generation, a selfish one, critics charged. Like all social experiments, ours was costly. Nevertheless, we know more of ourselves than we might have, and, in any event, we cannot go back. Writing is my way of going forward. This struggle to set down an integrated understanding of Alachua, to pull together my opposing experiences of country and town, placing them in historical and geographical perspective, is an effort to pierce the universal human difficulties common to all cultures: an attempt to understand the world.

Many of these chapters originated from notes taken in my car as I drove. I became a sort of traveling commentator, unconsciously part of an American tradition that includes such different writers as John Steinbeck, Charles Kuralt, James Agee, and Lillian Smith. For fifteen years I rode dirt back roads, seeking out our oldest rememberers in order to claim the childhood that boys were granted, but girls were not. Daddy hadn't thought it proper for a girl to go exploring on her own. I'd been overprotected. Although Daddy had taught me how to tighten the girth on a saddle, he customarily had his hired man ready the horse and hitch him to a fencepost near our farmhouse shortly before I got in from school. As an adult, I did learn the names of wildflowers and identify petrified bones from the bottom of the Santa Fe River, but eventually I realized I was stuck with the childhood I'd actually had. I saw, finally, the reality of my beginnings in a world that, however restricted physically and intellectually, was rich in stories and solitude, and I am grateful for that.

My written work is the thread of continuity in an unsettled life of many moves, changing allegiances, interstates from Mississippi to Florida, and dirt roads bordered by aged live oaks and kudzu. The work has never left me nor has it offered recriminations. It has never reduced my sense of self-worth. Writing returns ten times over whatever I invest, and it is always there when I come back to it. Pounding this keyboard, I move into the future.

This work emerged from a struggle to see my home community and myself in perspective. It took years, however, for me to realize that my formal research into the life of Alachua also served personal needs. While documenting Florida's Southern culture, I was simultaneously excavating my own familial foundations and cultural connections, struggling with the conflicting loyalties that came to be represented by a divided geography. A need to recognize and accept this ambivalence both motivated and sustained the work. Who I am is intrinsically entwined with place.

PART ONE:

THE COUNTRY

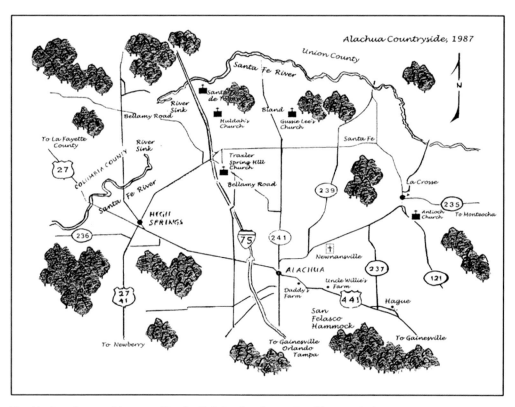

The Alachua Countryside, 1987. Map by Hal Cauthen (2006). Used by permission.

chapter 1:

Old Fields, Toadflax *(Alachua, Florida, 1987)*

Orion:	Don't think you'll ever fool with no more cows and hogs, huh?
Willie:	I know I won't, this foot and leg don't get better. I'll tell you, like you and me is now, it's shitty. Remember when we had something to look forward to every minute? Every half a day, yessir! Oh! Remember when that car hurt Allen? He was in the rest home . . . lay there unconscious.
Orion:	Thought he was gone die. Allen was driving. Sure thought for a long time old Allen wasn't going to make it.
Willie:	Well, I'll be dog! Oh, I'll tell you . . . a lot comes along, don't it?
Orion:	Uh, huh. Willie, I don't know how in the world Mama and Papa got through what they did, do you? It was just take and beg. That's all there was to it.
Willie:	Well, Papa always had a lot of chickens and hogs. And cows. We had pretty good calves and, you know, at that time it was a free range. That helped out a whole lot, don't you reckon?
Orion:	Oh, yeah . . .
Willie:	Papa, most any time, he had a *few* dollars in his pocket.
Orion:	Well, what is it Sudye wanta get . . . from Antioch [Cemetery] . . . all this stuff?
Willie:	Ain't no telling what . . . what she . . . ain't no telling what she wants with it.

—Orion and Willie Cauthen, April 1986[1]

After my father's death I cultivated relationships with two of his brothers, Orion and Willie, who were perplexed when I hammered them for details about the lives of family members buried at Antioch Cemetery. My uncles did not understand my hunger. They didn't realize that stories were the umbilical that tied me to home.

I like to joke that Alachua, the small Florida town I come from, is the kind of place where there's nothing much to see or do, but what you hear makes up for it. I'm tempted to say that talk and stories are what I came back for, but the truth is something more difficult than that.

I was away for fifteen years—college, marriage, motherhood—and, then, in the fall of 1975, just six months after my father died, I moved myself and my nine-year-old son, William, from Brevard County's Space Coast to a summer fishing cabin at a place called Waters Pond which some think naturalist William Bartram may have visited in 1774. Waters Pond is twenty-five miles west of Gainesville, in adjacent Gilchrist County, twenty miles from Alachua. After my father's death and a divorce in the space of one year, the water and the woods around it were balm, each morning's light on the pond a reminder that serenity is possible.

The little cabin had cracks we could look out through and, during dove hunting season, buckshot scattered like pecans on our tin roof. I had a job in nearby Gainesville, but couldn't live in the city for its noise. The whine of trucks on the interstate started me clenching my jaws, and even the traffic downtown made me jump—once into the path of a car. Waters Pond was cold, the neighbors silent and suspicious—their ways more "country" than those of my most primitive relatives—but it was beautiful and, when the hunters weren't there, silent.

Each afternoon, I picked up William from his Gainesville school and drove the twenty-five miles home as quickly as I could, racing toward the setting sun. Until Daylight Savings Time ended that fall, we had late afternoon tea and cookies—often in our overcoats—under a moss-draped oak at the edge of the water. Later, when William was in bed, I sat alone in the moonlight learning the phases of the moon. While I lived there, it seemed I could still hear my father's voice. He spoke whole sentences that hung in the air.

The cabin's one heater, fueled by bottled gas, threw out warmth enough for our hands and faces, then rose through the uninsulated ceiling and floated out over the pond. The heat merely took enough of the edge off the cold that we could bear to stay in the house. We had to turn the gas off while we slept or worry about carbon monoxide poisoning. The days just before Christmas were especially cold and one night, when we had been baking sheets of cookies with our coats on, William left the room. I finished up in the kitchen, and then found him. He was asleep under his electric blanket, still wearing boots, jacket, and wool hat.

It was lonely, but that felt about right. One Saturday morning when there was no gas to heat the place, we got in our yellow Volkswagen and drove into High Springs to what used to be called "the old Barber's Restaurant." We were sitting there, eating eggs and ham, and in came Norma Herndon Rayburn, a high school friend of my sister's who, like me, had divorced and come home with a child. Her girl was William's age. Norma came over to us and drawled, "Well, I can see you're back. But what I want to know is, what did you come back *for*?"

I must have said something about being interested in local history because, after we finished eating, Norma took us in her car out to the nearly impassable High Springs side of the Bellamy Road. Though local folks often reference "the Bellamy" when giving directions, and many know that a man from St. Augustine named John Bellamy widened the road early in the nineteenth century, people's accounts conflict. Many say he cleared the entire length of what is also known as "the old Spanish trail" that crosses Florida from St. Augustine to Pensacola but, in fact, Bellamy worked only the St. Augustine-Tallahassee portion. The U.S. Army cleared the rest. I'd never heard of the road prior to that cold Saturday morning, but I spent the next fifteen years driving it and similar dirt roads, Norma's question reverberating in my ears.

Waters Pond wasn't far from my mother's place, just back in the next county, but Mother wanted me closer. It took her two years to persuade me to move near her, into Alachua. Her efforts included choosing a house for us and arranging that Vada Beutke Horner, who would become my best friend, would give William a ride to his Gainesville school where, as it happened, Vada taught. For the entire spring semester of his fourth grade year, William rode to and from school in Vada's company, leaving me free to work at home. At the end of the school year, Vada would accept no pay for this—except for a pink box of dusting powder forced on her by my mother—and, after the school term ended, she continued to stop by. William went to live with his father the following year, but my friendship with Vada flourished.

In ten years, Vada taught me the names of all the flowering plants in my yard. Built in 1926 by the sawmill boss, George Duke, this is the most solidly constructed house I have ever lived in. Its dark wood trim and yellow pine floors are of premium lumber and, with their heavy paneled doors, each room is a sanctuary. Old Kate Haisten and her husband, Sam, who operated a grocery on Main Street for fifty years, bought the house from Duke. While Kate Haisten lived here, she planted narcissi and irises, star magnolias, Rubra and Professor Sargent camellias, Formosa azaleas, and crape myrtles. That's just the front yard. And now I am the house's lucky third owner.

When school lets out on Tuesdays, Vada and I go riding. She has been teaching first graders all day and I have been researching Florida history, so it is a relief to get in the car and head for those winding overgrown dirt roads around this place, Alachua. Our choice of roads is instinctual; we are hunting for stories and, like the early European explorers, we don't know what we will find. A map like the sixteenth-century De Soto Map suffices, for its Florida is suggestive, elusive, as riveting as the soft thuds of my unborn sister's heartbeat when I was three, as mysterious as the folded unknowns of my mother's body against which I pressed my ear. The De Soto Map does not tell; it beckons.

Once a week, Vada and I drive together and, in between, I drive alone—mornings, with coffee and country music, and evenings, with Jack Daniels in a pint Mason jar. I am compelled to get in the car and investigate the unmarked and little-known roads that separate green fields of growing crops. There is something I have to find and, though I cannot name it, I am certain it is here, somewhere, in these green woods. I can feel its pull, as real and strong as Prince, the horse I rode as a girl.

You cannot know a place unless you drive its roads in a leisurely way, open to possibilities—the flashing ribbon of a red fox, the papery peelings of a river birch's trunk, the two-inch face of an intricate passionflower, peeping from the roadside. People who rush miss all of this, seeing only woods and weeds, but the

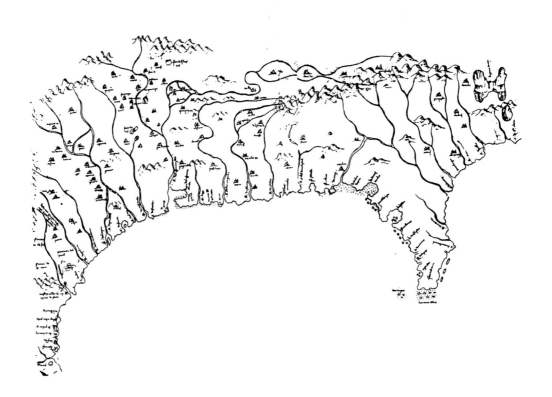

The "De Soto Map" or Route of the De Soto Expedition, circa 1544.[2]

7

places we live in and thoughtfully travel through yield themselves to us, as a person does, when we take the time.

One day, I took my sister, Emily, who lives in Orlando and says she would never come back to live in Alachua, on a drive to Waters Pond. We followed the road I was driving five days a week to and from my job in Gainesville. Rushing home after work, I never had the leisure to investigate side roads so, by the time Emily and I were ten miles out of Gainesville, I must have wandered off the main highway a dozen times, saying, "Let's go just a mile over" or "Let's see whether or not there's a stream running through those trees."

Once, I stopped to admire the bark of a gnarled cedar tree, cut off the engine, and pointed out to Emily what an artist friend had shown me: the tree's bark was not brown or gray, but a dozen flecks of color. Unexamined, it looked gray. "Can't we please just go straight to Waters Pond?" Emily asked. I answered, "Yes, we can," and then, about a mile further up the road, I reflexively turned again. Emily's eyes widened and she said, with what I remember as resignation and disapproval, "Well! I believe you're like Daddy. He would go down a road just because it was there."

Emily and I were driving near where our Cauthen, Goolsby, Colson, and Mott kin had traveled on their way out from the Carolinas and Georgia, when Alachua County's original boundaries stretched from the Georgia line on the north to Port Charlotte Harbor, 100 miles south of present-day Tampa. And they did not always follow along roads, but cut through woods and forded rivers and streams. I think maybe what is real for Emily is what is right in front of her, but that has never been true for me. It's what is under, behind, or right around the other side of the thing in front of me: that's what I'm searching for. Looking into these lush woods, I can imagine our ancestors—women and men with their children—picking out a path with stout walking poles, pulling their animals along on leads.

The year before my father died, I completed a college degree, my studies spread out over fourteen years. For a linguistics course called "Black English," I recorded Daddy's speech. In bed with emphysema, he made a ready, captive informant. Daddy was white, but in his "Cracker" language I detected black dialect markers as he talked about growing up in the countryside near an old African-American settlement called Monteocha. I taped stories of his red-harnessed pet goat pulling him and his brothers around the farm in a wagon; about his brother, Willie, trading the other five boys out of their biddies and hiding the baby chicks under the family's board-and-batten house that Granddaddy Cauthen set up off the ground on stones dug out of the fields he farmed. Since I live with these busy ghosts, I want to find out more about them. Vada, who lives in her grandmother's old house on the family farm, feels their closeness, too.

Vada and I are living not only in the present, but simultaneously in the many periods during which the stories of our ancestors are set. Her people and mine have been in Alachua for five generations; mine arrived before Florida gained statehood in 1845. We are grown women in our forties, but, like children hunting treasure, we are determinedly scouring out our histories, following one clue at a time.

In our travels, we often drive northwest of the City of Alachua, along a section of the Bellamy Road opened with slave labor in the early 1800s. On this road, from inside a lush green tunnel walled and roofed by spreading, ancient oaks, we envision Spanish missionaries and, earlier, the Native Americans who padded on foot long before their dirt path became the Spanish Trail which stretches to California; we see Florida's earliest pioneers (during the Territorial Period, 1821–1845) before the federal government paid John Bellamy to widen the route from St. Augustine to Tallahassee for settlers' wagons, enticing pioneer families to brave snakes and mosquitoes in Florida.[3]

Besides putting details of flora and fauna and bits of old people's stories into fiction, I am keeping a journal I call *One More Time*. This title comes from what Daddy's sister, Nadine, said when I called her in Nokomis, in South Florida, to tell her he had died. "Oh, no!" my aunt said, "I wanted to talk with him, just one more time." Being back in Alachua is like that, like watching a loved relative die, bit by bit. Both Vada and I know that what we search for is being buried under asphalt, concrete, and steel faster than we can get at it.

On an early spring afternoon, we leave the Bellamy near Bland and turn, clockwise, toward the town of Santa Fe, traveling through an area labeled on our yellowed map, "Old Fields." White-faced Hereford cattle graze in the pastures we pass as we move in a long, slow turn, circling the town.

At Santa Fe, we pass the house where, in 1958, my Uncle Colson killed himself. I have always been haunted by Mother's only brother, Colson, who, as a young sailor on leave during World War II, held me on his lap and told me stories of faraway places while I traced the swirling patterns of the blue tattoos that covered his arms. When I get desperate, I think about how invisible traits, as well as the color of hair and the shape of eyes, also get passed on in a family.

Today, in a ditch near Uncle Colson's former home stand four migrant workers. As a child I was taught to label "Mexican" the straight, black hair and exotic brown faces of schoolchildren who arrived with their families in the spring of each year, to disappear come fall. These four men are as still as statues, turning only their eyes as we drive past, and my first thought is that they are staring because they feel as I do. I am startled by the realization that they never knew Uncle Colson. They do not know the significance of the old, unpainted house and its empty windows glinting like eyes from either side of the front door. For them, the house doesn't call up images. They have no idea those random creaks in the night are the footsteps of my uncle's ghost. The men stand like figures in a frieze, tiny details framing and calling attention to a larger story. They are merely unknowing witnesses. And they are not staring; I am.

He has been dead for thirty years, yet Uncle Colson's house still poses questions: what kind of place is this, this town of Santa Fe, and how terrible can life get that a man should lie down in his bedroom, use his big toe to pull the trigger on his stepson's rifle, and put a bullet into his own head? I have talked with the nurse who accompanied the doctor who signed the death certificate; she told me what she saw, how the body looked. I also know Colson had cancer of the throat and sclerosis of the liver; he was an alcoholic. But I cannot fathom what he must have thought that morning after the children and his wife were gone, what he saw last, what final phrase went through his head.

Within an hour of his death, my grandmother who, since before sunrise, had been fishing in the Gulf of Mexico 300 miles away, mouthed to my step-grandfather over the roar of their outboard motor, "Something's happened to Colson." By the time they tied up the fishing boat at their dock, my mother's telegram was flapping on the back door.

I don't tell Vada that I am thinking about my uncle, remembering that the preacher's wife came and got me from school that day and took me to the Baptist pastorium, how I waited there for Mother. Until then, I always thought of Daddy, who was a binge drinker, as the unstable one, but Mother's people include a cousin who served time at Raiford, the state penitentiary, and an uncle who wrote hate letters to Alachua General Hospital complaining of having been served food there by a Negro. Both these men were Mama's Colson kin.

Then there is also Mama's own father, Samuel Hill Meggs, who stepped—or was pushed—off a moving train on his way home from work in 1910. His body was found beside the railroad tracks in a field, here in Santa Fe, not more than a mile from where his only son, Colson, would also die violently forty-seven years later. No explanation; Mama does not want to talk about it. All I have been able to learn of my grandfather's death is what Aunt Nancy told me in her oral history about the horse-drawn hearse and my mother's reactions to it.

I once shouted at my mother that I would kill myself if I could figure out how to make it look like an accident. I must have known intuitively the effect my words might have on her, for she suffered terribly over Uncle Colson's death. Again and again, all that long year after he died, she woke up screaming. Once, in the middle of the night, we both woke up: she was dreaming of Colson's death, and I, of hers.

Colson's grown stepson has said that, in spite of the beatings my uncle gave him, he loved the man as his own father. He told me about coming home from school that day to find his father a suicide and learning that the gun Colson had used was his, a boy's gun. I shuddered because, as he related the grim details, the stepson was polishing to a mirror-like shine the boots, pistol, and the barrel of the rifle he uses every day as a deputy sheriff.

I never mention any of this to Vada as we drive. For all Vada knows, I am simply admiring the details of landscape as we roam about Santa Fe, taking in its dozen varieties of new green. The stands of pecan trees are all budding out. In Alachua, people say the pecan is the last tree to unfold its blossoms in spring and, when it does, winter is finished.

At the edge of town, we tramp through what Mama's oldest friend, Emery Williams, would have described as "worlds" of vines and briers, while Vada explains to me the distinctions between flowering dewberry and flowering blackberry, which both have thorns and look so much alike I cannot tell the difference. Vada, still wearing her schoolteaching dress and high-heeled shoes, leads the way to a grown-over cemetery in the woods behind Mebane School. This burying place was once accessible by car and, earlier, the footpath past it was probably a loop in the Bellamy Road. The loop is lost, the cemetery obscured since Mebane was built—as an appeasement to Blacks—in advance of a planned "white" school, an effort to forestall integration in the early 1950s. The small cemetery, like the pond beyond it, is tangible local history. Although lynched bodies dangling above the pond from tree limbs are seldom mentioned, that spot of water is commonly called Gallows Pond.

Above an eye-level growth of vines and briers, we spot a fat tree that dwarfs the small graveyard, a giant camellia that once each year spatters the tombstones with thick, pink petals. They are dropping as we approach. All of the stones are broken, but Vada and I collect enough pieces to spell out "Maggie" from a marker that six months ago was intact. Local vandals also visit regularly.

As Vada leads me out of the woods, I ask if she plans ever to wear that particular pair of nylon stockings again. She just laughs, points out the creamy rosettes of the Spanish bayonet, the plant whose sharp, pointed lengths my childhood playmates and I brandished as swords, and goes on thrashing through the underbrush like a modern-day conquistador.

It is easy to envision conquistadors in these woods, because they were once here. The town, Santa Fe, took its name from an early Spanish mission named much earlier than places in the American West called "Santa Fe" (possibly a corruption of "holy faith"). Many people have heard of Florida's Ponce de Leon and the story of his search for the Fountain of Youth, but few know that Pedro Mendendez celebrated a mass with Indians of the Seloy Tribe at St. Augustine in 1565, fifty-five years before the Pilgrims landed at Plymouth Rock.

Vada and I make our last stop of the day near Santa Fe, at St. John's Methodist Church. I was here once, years ago, but never have been able to find my way back. In front of the church door the ground is swept clean, like the rural yards where people brush away leaves and loose trash with their brooms, so that only a shining dirt pan shows.

We wander over to the cemetery to look for two gravestones with amazing names: Susan Atlanta Ellis and Osceola Van Ellis, a sister and brother whose parents gave them names like chapter titles for the history of this place. Confederate crosses in our cemeteries—at Newnansville (first called "Dell's Post Office"), Antioch, where my Cauthen grandparents are buried, and in small family plots by the side of the road—memorialize ancestors who died in the American Civil War. On markers grown over with gray lichen are the names of relatives who, in the 1800s, defended Fort Gilliland, said to have been attacked by the Florida Seminole leader, Osceola, and his followers who came on horseback through these woods. That fort no longer stands. And the graves of the aboriginal Timucuans who met the conquistadors of the 1500s are deep underground.[4]

This past week, I have been sifting sand with an archaeologist searching for the lost Spanish mission of Santa Fe de Toloca, believed to be somewhere near here, but I witnessed my first archaeological dig in Ireland, a few years ago. I and other students at the William Butler Yeats International Summer School watched as a scientist explained the procedures used to reclaim history, layer by layer. In studying bits of chert and bone, Vada and I are, like archaeologists, imaginatively reconstructing the Civil War, the Indian Wars, and the lives of the Timucuans.

When Vada backs the car away from the front of the church steps, a pile of white stones comes into view. The pile looks much like a miniature dolmen,

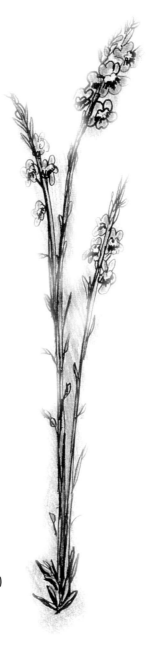

Toadflax (*Linaria canadensis*). Drawing (2002)
© Janet Moses. Used by permission.

one of the mysterious megalithic constructions I saw in Ireland. Dolmens, constructed of enormous stones, are reminders of Stonehenge, calling up images of prehistoric peoples ritually reenacting their hopes and dreams.

On my trip to Ireland, the introduction to archaeology was incidental. I had crossed the Atlantic with one motive: to lay flowers on the grave of W. B. Yeats, paying homage to the man whose poems were the last thing I read each night since my father's death, before I turned off my bedside lamp.

I had not wanted to share my first sight of Yeats's grave with 500 of my fellow students at the Yeats Summer School, so I left the cries of heron and gull on Sligo Bay behind and hiked alone the five miles uphill to Drumcliffe Churchyard. I stamped along in a steady mist too gentle to be called rain, and so slowly that I began really to see wildflowers for the first time. As I walked, I picked samples of each curious flower that appeared along my path: pink roses from a rock fence behind which red cattle grazed, blue harebells in sheltered spots, purple thistles starting like feathers out of smooth hard globes, and the pale blossoms of wild blackberry. That walk made me a devotee of wildflowers.

My favorite of Yeats's lines are from a poem called, "A Dialogue of Self and Soul":

> I am content to follow to its source
> Every event in action or in thought;
> Measure the lot; forgive myself the lot!
> When such as I cast out remorse
> So great a sweetness flows into the breast
> We must laugh and we must sing,
> We are blest by everything,
> Everything we look upon is blest.[5]

I still say those lines to myself, only now I know why they were so important in 1975. The word "blest" wasn't yet in my vocabulary; it described the emotional destination I unconsciously yearned for.

As Vada and I leave St. John's Church, large lilac shadows speed at us, puddles of color on the shoulders of the road. As we approach, the puddles, like pointillist paintings, separate into thousands of delicate toadflax (*Linaria canadensis*), their fragile heads curled over and down, nodding, wave-like, in the wind. Most people who see toadflax dismiss it as a weed, but it belongs to the Scrophulariaceae family, which includes the more showy foxglove and snapdragon. Toadflax flowers are only one-fourth to one-half inch long, with five sepals each. The upper lip of the flower has two lobes and the lower lip has three, each with two small, white ridges. If you look closely, you see a mouth that is open and moveable.

Vada pulls over and stops. I get out, choose just one flower, and bring it back to the car. We sit for a while, pinching its blue lips open and closed, watching its mouth move.

Right on the Land *(Alachua, Florida, 1988)*

> Most important to us was that we keep the farm going, and my father
> said to me about two weeks before he died, "Mary Lou, do with the farm
> just like you want to do." Oh, it was the most wonderful thing to be able
> to do it and still live. And right now I am crocheting almost every
> minute I get a waking hour. Cause Sister and I are slipping; we know.
> We know we're both slipping but, still, life is still worth living and
> it's wonderful to be able to do something, some little something
> for somebody else.
>
> —Mary Lou McFadden, July 1987[1]

At the south end of Alachua County, Marjorie Kinnan Rawlings, writing
Cross Creek in 1942, declared that something withers in a man when he is out of
touch with the soil.[2] Nothing she wrote is more central to my own belief; it seems
to me there is a wholeness in the rural people of Alachua that comes from their
everyday knowledge of the earth and the way they pace their lives to its rhythms.
They accept change as natural, and they are on good terms with death. The
farmers furnish some of what I lost when I disowned Alachua and moved away
and they are so at peace with their lives that, when I'm with them, I grow content
about my own. Walking their furrowed fields, picking beans, listening to their
talk about whether the river is too low or too high, brings back my childhood
connection with the land.

Our farm was sold years ago when Daddy got too sick to work it, but in the countryside around Alachua I am finding again the lost bits and pieces of my childhood and creating an extended family for myself. The sisters Mary Lou McFadden and Vernon McFadden Hill—both in their late eighties— are part of that family. I go often to visit Mary Lou and Vernon, sometimes alone, sometimes with Vada. Because they cannot hear well enough to talk on the phone, we seldom call to tell them we are coming. Their dog alerts them as Vada and I swing up the driveway; by the time we park and get out, Mary Lou is waving from the front door of their mobile home and Vernon from the back.

They have not always lived in the mobile home on their nephew's place. The women moved there two years ago after the farmhouse they grew up in burned. It was an old house full of memories, wardrobes of clothing, carved furniture, and delicate dishes. Every catalog Sears ever published was in the attic and gnarled viburnum and fig trees had grown up against the house and covered the ground in long curls. The sisters are stoics, but "before the house burned" now finds a place in all their stories; since the fire broke their hearts, nothing has been the same. In one brief Sunday morning they lost their privacy, their independence, and the beds they slept in.

In a January 1983 Sunday newspaper feature on the fire, Mary Lou and Vernon are pictured exclaiming over a pink bud on a rosebush in front of a backdrop of smoke and a mammoth pile of burnt sticks. The man who set the fire had worked for the family all of his life but, that day, he was angry with Mary Lou about the way she had ordered him to pick up pecans. He said he "didn't mean to burn nothing but just the couch." However, he lost control of his small blaze and it consumed the house. He went to prison and, although the sisters tell the story again and again, they always leave out his name.

Today, hundreds of red poppy mallows flap on the shoulder of the highway where Vada turns under the heavy leaning limbs of a giant oak, its curves echoing those in the dirt lane ahead. The double row of oaks marching northward, as well as artifacts discovered a mile away, suggests this may be where Hernando de Soto crossed in 1539 on his way through Florida toward the lost Timucuan Indian village of Cholupaha.

As we drive up the road, Mary Lou is telling Vada a folkloric account of the

Queen of England and her consort driving through in wagons more than 100 years ago, and Vernon is pointing out the house where John Bellamy stayed. Mary Lou turns in her seat, interrupting her own recital to make sure Vernon's is complete. "John Bellamy," she says, "went barefoot and wore a palmetto hat."

"Until," Vernon volleys back, "his horse ate the hat."

In the rear view mirror, Vada's eyes meet mine, acknowledging our continuing delight in these two storytellers. Mary Lou resettles herself in her seat, satisfied. We enter the clearing and see what is left of the house, a shell commemorating fire and malice. Charred pages from a photograph album flutter across the ground. Each picture was a story. Through these pictures Mary Lou and Vernon first began telling me their histories ten years ago, over glasses of iced tea on the front porch. Now the pictures, except for two or three rescued from the coals, are lost. The skeleton of their mother's tall oak marriage bed stands in the front room, a drift of leaves covering its blackened springs.

Mary Lou and Vernon give the house only a glance before plunging off into weeds higher than their heads. Although she has a bad hip "from where the tractor rolled over on me," Mary Lou is moving quickly toward what remains of the little vineyard she planted in Scuppernong grapes a few years ago. I follow, thinking we are all moving through the overgrowth in the same direction, but then, in the bushes behind me, I hear Vernon's wondering voice exclaim, "I've found me a peach!" Mary Lou, already past the peaches, throws back, "There's a few there, but they look mighty ornery." Vada chuckles. Mindful of our responsibility for the two women, she scrambles ahead to Mary Lou, muttering, "She's going to get in that poison ivy like she did last time."

At eighty-eight, Mary Lou no longer drives the tractor (though a few years ago I coaxed her into driving it down Gainesville's University Avenue hauling a straw-filled flatbed with two guitarists, a banjo player, a bulldog, and my son, William, under the Alachua County Folk Arts banner), nor is Vernon as active as she once was. Nevertheless, their enthusiasm for growing things is unchanged. In spite of disappointments—none worse than the fire—they still follow the examples of their family's pioneer life: they "make do" for, as Mary Lou says, "things present themselves."

"Grandpa John" Hollingsworth McFadden, a California forty-niner, used the gold he panned to buy land in Florida, purchasing unseen what he thought were a fine house and citrus groves. After the family arrived by train from Kentucky and walked six miles along a deserted dirt road, they came upon their purchase of eight bent orange trees and "a house with windows so dirty you couldn't tell daylight from dark on the inside." Cheated of orange groves, they learned to farm.

Mary Lou earned her first dollar in 1910, picking 100 pounds of cotton, and vividly she narrates the arrival of the boll weevil. "A little, teeny black bug," Vernon interjects. In order to eradicate the insect, growers were forced to set their cotton afire. McFadden cotton income was reduced from $8,000 in 1917, to $500 in 1918. The extent of the devastation caused by the boll weevil is evidenced by the volumes of songs, legends, jokes, and stories it inspired. Mr. Emery Williams, who was a living, walking history book, said:

> The whole countryside was based on cotton. There were about
> five cotton gins right here in Alachua. Two or three right here
> in town, big gins. But the boll weevil cut all that out. And there
> was a town up here in South Georgia that built a monument and
> put a boll weevil on top of it. The people found out they could
> make a living doing something else and, in a way, it was the best
> thing that ever happened to them.[3]

After the weevil's destruction, Alachua County farmers turned their efforts to the production of tobacco, cattle, and vegetables. These days, the local tobacco industry is imperiled. Although most growers have modernized their operations with mechanical harvesters and have replaced old wooden barns with modern metal ones for curing, many farmers discuss the anti-smoking lobby in tones of anger and fear. They produce less tobacco each year.

After their father's death in 1956, Vernon, widowed by then, joined Mary

Lou on the farm, following their father's late-life injunction to "run things." They were fifty-two and fifty-four, but they matter-of-factly took over all the work and management of the farm. They also purchased more acreage.

Asked about role models for women when she was a girl, Mary Lou responds: "Grandmother McFadden, she and I'd go pick blackberries, and one day—she wore her skirts real long—we were picking blackberries and a big snake crawled out between her feet. She didn't do a thing but kick him out of the way. She went right on picking blackberries. My father's mother!"

They remember their grandmother growing into old age, "with a *Bible* on her lap. She believed it. Our grandfather made Papa read ten chapters of the *Bible* every Sunday morning before he went to church. He was a man of that type." He was also a son who each morning went out and "checked for the smoke rising a mile away from his mother's chimney."

Church was (and still remains) important, and even the plowing of fields was interrupted for it. When the hour arrived to leave for weekly women's meetings at the Mikesville Presbyterian Church, Vernon tells that she would "drive the car to the edge of the field and stop." Mary Lou continues: "I got down from the tractor and climbed over the fence. After the meeting, Sister dropped me off and I went back to plowing again."

Leaving the burned farm, we travel a twisting dirt road that stops abruptly at a thin wall of trees. Beyond the trees is a fast-moving line of cars on Interstate 75 which, twenty-eight years ago, cut the Bellamy Road in half. The road continues on the opposite side of the interstate and can be reached only by retracing our path and circling back over the interchange. Parked facing the line of trees with the engine turned off, Vada and I ignore the traffic and reenter with the sisters, via their stories, the world of their schooldays: the one-room school they walked to, the country store at Traxler where they bought jawbreaker candies in the afternoons, and the cemetery where tall monuments still stand at the heads of their Hollingsworth grandparents' graves. When the sisters grow quiet, Vada starts the car.

On the way back, Mary Lou and Vernon point out various crops. Vada, who plants vegetables every year, knows them all already, including the low green rows of bushes on which bell-shaped peppers are turning red. After all the crops are named, Mary Lou is silent, but Vernon is explaining the "widow's club" the two sisters belong to. I ask questions about requirements for membership because, after all, Mary Lou never married.

"Mary Lou, how long we been in the widows' club?" asks Vernon. Mary Lou rasps out, "Since 1966," her eyes never leaving the line of red peppers.

"But how could Mary Lou get in?" I whisper. Vada, watching me in the rear view mirror, presses her lips tightly together in merriment. Vernon throws her head back and laughs. "Oh, she's honorary."

The sun is dropping in the sky when we return to the mobile home. Mary Lou flips on the lights when she goes in the door, sits, and resumes talk of farming while, with the knitting needles she has taken up, she converts a skein of red wool into one more of the hundreds of caps she gives away to neighbors and visitors. Vernon picks up her lace tatting shuttle and goes to work, too.

I hope next spring they will still have energy enough to cultivate their small patches of tomatoes and beans beside the mobile home. I hope they will still look out through the windows and follow the turning, furrowing, and planting of the soil, note the height of new plants, the rainfall; see the crescent moon grow fat, then wane.

On days when the weather is good and they feel well enough, Mary Lou and Vernon walk the perimeters of their nephew's property, talking of other years and other crops; taking in the sight and scent of every growing thing. Mary Lou tells me walking is an activity she means to continue, "until we get to drop like Papa, right on the land."

c h a p t e r   3:

Locusts and Wild Honey (*Traxler, Florida, 1988*)

> We worked outdoors. My husband was a farmer-preacher, we raised
> everything: hogs, sows, chickens, ducks, and turkeys, and guineas.
> My family was raised, we ate at home. Because my husband planted
> something each month in the year, it was always something coming up
> to go on the table. A lot of people ask me, "How did you manage to feed
> all these children when there was fifteen heads sitting at the table
> three times a day?" I have cooked twelve cakes of cornbread on top
> of the stove, and I did not even get a piece!
> —Letha Wright DeCoursey, 1983[1]

Just down the road from the old McFadden place, near what remains of the
Traxler cotton gin, the chatter of a pair of cardinals is broken by the racket of
trucks from the interstate. Here, on a cool summer morning, in the stillness of
weeds and dilapidated buildings, memory speaks.

From 1880 until 1920, Traxler, with its complex of gin, gristmill, and
commissary, was one of the countryside's hubs of commerce, a rural precursor
to the shopping center. Families brought their cotton here to be ginned and
their corn to be ground and, whether they made purchases or not, they lingered,
surveying the bolts of colored cloth, jawbreaker candies, and harmonicas in the
commissary.

Lucile Skinner Traxler, who married into the family and is the last of its
members living here, came from nearby Newberry in 1937 to teach in the

community's one-room school. "There were five or six clerks working at one time in that store," Mrs. Traxler says. Each year, her future father-in-law went to Boston, New York City, Baltimore, and Savannah on the Clyde boat line to sell cotton. The commissary was also a post office, with a slot in its door for the deposit of outgoing mail during hours when the store was closed.

I prowl Traxler alone, intent, trying to see it busy again. A nubby lichen grows between cracks in the gin's half-open cypress doors. The doors, weathered into grays, mauves, and greens, have sunk into the ground and will not open any further; attempts to push them forward or backward merely lift the rotting lumber away from the frame.

On the ground inside is half of a leather shoe sole, like the ones on my Daddy's boots that I unlaced when he came in from the fields. A section of a horse bridle studded with brass lies where the mules stood hitched to wagons, waiting while each load of cotton was weighed. The weighing floor where the mules stood has disappeared.

Some of the boards in this structure are marked with chalk. Over wet, green algae, the letters and numbers are difficult to read. Each board is marked separately so that the gin can be exactly reconstructed. The historic preservation team, crating what is left of the building for the Florida Agricultural Museum in Tallahassee, says this is the best remaining example of the cotton gin so central to North Florida's development. Grayed bits of cotton cling to gears that last turned more than sixty years ago and clumped between the brushes that combed raw fibers. A black debris fills the spaces between the serrated edges of toothed metal wheels that extracted seeds.

The museum's technician has removed a portion of one wall. Looking through the opening, I see lying on the ground an immense iron part resembling a corkscrew that must weigh as much as a compact car. It has fallen through the rotten third floor, then the second.

Spiders have webbed the second floor window openings flanked by sagging shutters. Against the roughened walls, grape vines thick as pencils dry in stiff curls. A rusted hopper lies with its lid thrown open and, into its open mouth, a line of rain drips from the tin roof's edge. This cypress building reminds me of the barns where my father and his father stored their corn and hay.

Nearby, an oyster-white lichen creeps up the side of a reclining chair abandoned under the reddening arms of a stout oak. Stuffing spills from the chair's covered arms, the rotting fabric reminiscent of the smell in my playhouse when I left it closed one hot, rainy summer and the faces of all my rubber dolls melted. I have heard Mrs. Traxler's, as well as Mary Lou and Vernon's, stories about these ruins. One of the most intriguing conversations I had was with Letha DeCoursey.

Letha Wright DeCoursey, the granddaughter of an emancipated slave, was born in 1899. Letha remembers going to work with her mother, Palaice, who worked for the Traxler family. "After she'd cook the dinner, set the table, and feed the white folks, then she set me up on a tin pan to make me high enough for the table, and give me dinner." Palaice also worked at the cotton gin where black drivers unloaded cotton wagons while farmers following their crop yields watched from horse-drawn buggies. Letha saw the piles of cotton with a child's eyes: "The first time I seen 'em, I thought they was a mountain." During harvest time, the line of waiting wagons was a long, white streak that stretched from the gin all the way down the road, past Springhill Church where Letha's ancestors worshipped with whites.

Picking cotton was laborious, Letha says.

> Backbreaking and fingersnagging. I had a brother and a sister could pick a hundred pounds of cotton a day. They could pick with two hands. And, my brother, he could carry two rows. Both hands. And if the cotton was scattered and he couldn't carry but one row, then he would always straddle that row, bushes and all, and go with his sack draggin' behind him.

Workers sang "field hollers to keep the spirit up." In a low, mellow voice, Letha demonstrates:

> Down in the bot-tom
> Where the cot-ton
> Waaas rot-ten
> Now layyyyyyyyyyyy
> Five fingers in the boll.

Although some of her aunts and uncles could pick 200 or even 300 pounds of cotton in a day, Letha reports, "They never made a cotton picker out of me. They would whip me in the field because I'd hold onto the boll to pick the cotton out. They said, 'Letha, you're just teasin the cotton out of that boll.'"

The top step of the arched entrance to Springhill Church has bowed in, as though the combined weight of all the Methodists who have entered it since it first opened its doors in the 1860s had been set down on it at once. Slender rectangles of stained glass dedicated to members of the Dell family, the area's oldest, hang on both walls of the covered entrance.

The double chocolate-brown doors to the sanctuary are always unlocked. I open them and, just inside, the lower shelf of a footed table holds wooden-handled cardboard fans, like the ones people waved in front of their faces during summer church revivals before air conditioning. On the top shelf, an open scrapbook bulges with clippings, photographs, and mementos, all displayed on a hand-crocheted cloth. An 1897 McFadden wedding: the women wear long black skirts and high white blouses and their hair pulled straight back. I wonder if, under those skirts, they buttoned up high-topped shoes.

The first time I was in this church, I came for a wedding. The bride floated down the aisle in a glory of white tulle and golden hair, her eyes as blue as the Virgin's. Though divorced, I still believed that marriage was not only possible, but possible for me. Looking as though they saw only the truths behind each other's eyes, and not the church packed with witnesses, nor the minister in front of them, the young couple said their vows in trembly voices. I came back alone and found a church that, even without bridal finery, impressed its indelible shapes and colors on my memory. I came to know its sanctuary in weekday silence, and the look of rain through the wavy glass windows of its Sunday School rooms. Once I came on a Monday and found an Easter cross on the lawn. Cultivated lilies, field phlox, roses, and wild violets like Mother and I once picked at Burnett's Lake had been fastened together. I imagined children being lifted up by their parents to pin on bouquets, and then set down to stand before the cross, admiringly, with all their church family.[2]

Empty, the church is a simplicity of stained glass, white walls, and red carpet, a church a movie might be set in, one about people connected by something more than geography or accident of birth, a family who knows its connection in a depth beyond telling. In spite of its bright colors, Springhill is a plain, country church where one can easily imagine that, of all scripture, the words of the Beatitudes most belong. It is a place where even a stranger can pray. "Blessed are the poor in spirit," one might begin.[3]

During antebellum days, slaves entered the church building through a back door. The pulpit stood in the middle of the room. The wooden pews were hand-hewn by slaves for the original building. Beneath the lacquer, my fingers detect the ridged grain of these pews. Under the shiny surface, bumps and cuts in the wood suggest a planing tool not sharp enough, or a workman hitting against the grain, lifting his tool, and starting again. Many slaves were buried in and around the present graveyard, but those graves are not marked. If they once had markers, they have rotted away.

On an earlier visit to the cemetery, Letha and I discussed her grandfather, Brisker Blue, who died in 1910 when he was 115 years old and Letha was eleven. He came from Africa as a boy, lived on the Hodge Plantation where remnants of a slave cemetery can still be seen, a short distance from here. He may have helped carve these benches and hammer their backs on with square nails. He may have entered through the back door and taken his seat in this very pew.

Letha remembers Brisker Blue as "a workin' old man. On the farm, cleanin' up the ground, cuttin' wood. Whenever the Freedom come out he stayed on at the Hodge Plantation. He never owned land of his own."

In the damp and silent graveyard, red mushrooms are scattered on the ground under live oak trees. The live oaks are old, their limbs covered with resurrection ferns as thick as beards. The end of one rotting wood plank sticks up from the grass with no name on it. In the back of the cemetery, two colonies of algae partially obscure the carved leaves and crosses of a Celtic design on a tall, granite monument. One colony is green. The other, gray-blue as any spring water, looks like a design shaping and reshaping itself into a galaxy of stars.

One wide double marker with a man's birth and death dates on the left reads, "Hunnicutt." On the right, only a woman's first name: "Ithiel." Letha explained that Ithiel was her childhood playmate, a white girl whose mother had befriended Letha's mother, Palaice Wright.

The air was sweetly fragrant that day, and Letha pointed out the pink, hairy blossoms of a mimosa tree. Waving one finger toward the tree, she said, "I knows that as a 'locust'. Accordin' to the *Bible*, that was John the Baptist's food, when he in the desert. Locusts and wild honey!"[4]

In addition to her employment with the Traxlers, Letha's mother was also a midwife and herbalist who scouted the woods with Letha at her side and taught her daughter to concoct remedies from snakeroot and elderberry. The tree commonly called mimosa (*Albizia julibrissin*) is a member of the Leguminosae family, which includes beans and peas. The plant originated in the Old World and in 1745 was introduced into the southern United States where it is now common.

Near the mimosa arching from the overgrowth adjacent to the clearing where Spring Hill Church sits, Letha spotted a ground cover whose blossoms closely resemble the mimosa's, walked over to it, bent down, and—as the plant's leaves, in response to her touch, curled inward—whispered "shameface."

While Palaice harvested herbs with a hoe and a hatchet not far from present-day Alachua, it was Letha's task to "tote beside her" the bolls, berries, and bark

28

they collected. Much of the wild hammock where they found medicinal plants such as "Christeverlasting" and "Devil's Shoestring" has been cleared for farms, cut through by highways, and carved into today's City of Alachua. Only the occasional giant oak standing on private property confirms Letha's description of the land as it once was and a way of life where virtually nothing was useless:

This was open, no fence laws. Them cows would go out in the woods and die. You find a cow and people would be just as busy watching that old carcass, and when the buzzard got through with it, them old bones looked like they was about to dry. Oh, I've toted many a stack of bones—old cow foots, cow legs, and cow hips, and whatnots. Oh, you'd take them and take an axe and chop 'em up. Put 'em in that wash pot out there and build a fire and boil 'em and you'd be surprised the grease that would come out of them bones.

My mama make us get the foots. You see, [people] throwed all that away. The cow head, too. Now, a cow foot have a artery in it and that old artery's good for more than one thing. When children used to have whooping cough you take that cow foot artery, cook it out to where there weren't no water in it: it's just as clear and [when] you have children with the whooping cough they took it just like they took castor oil. [For] a little baby, you take a thick cloth and wet it in that meat foot oil and put just a slight kerosene and just pin it on the baby's shirt. If he had any chest cold back there, between the shoulders, it'll sneeze, come out in chunks. Cough it up.

Letha treated the children of others as well as her own. She frequently used pine rosin and elderberry in herbal remedies for rash, constipation, arthritis, "swellings," bedsores, diabetes; for healing the stumps of amputated limbs; for prickly heat, chicken pox, whooping cough, chest colds, worms, asthma, backache, and kidney trouble. When her daughter had something called "dango fever," Letha boiled a weed called "yeller gal."

Measles, like any other condition, was treated with something near at hand:

> You ain't got a thing to do but go out there and get you some shucks out
> the barn, shucks off the corn, dry corn shucks. Put 'em in a pot and boil
> 'em. Make a tea. Put you a little sugar in it, if you want it. Drink it cold
> if you want it cold. Drink it hot. Give him a cup of shuck tea tonight
> and put him to bed. You see, his temperature gonna rise. When he get up
> in the morning, his measles is all over.[5]

On the front lawn of Springhill Church, we stood together, looking back at
the old commissary where Letha had stood as a little girl, squinting down a line
of cotton wagons toward the church. She saw the gin when its parts moved, never
dreaming that one day she would walk about its broken-down building, drawing
pictures in the air with her fingers to show horses and buggies and cotton wagons
pulled by mules. She never imagined the place would fall silent for thirty years,
then have its quiet broken not by the old familiar sounds, but by an interstate's roar.

Time has dropped an illustrator's acetate overlay over Traxler. The picture
appears dark, still, and silent; but lift the overlay and Letha's line of wagons starts
up and lurches forward, one wagon at a time. Bales of white cotton replace the
broken recliner chair and Letha, young again, stands in the road holding in her
small hands a large cookie, a treat that cost one penny at the commissary. She
raises it to her mouth: "A cookie large enough for any five-year-old child." I see
her standing there, in 1904, steadily chewing, watching the life of Traxler swirl
about her. With her, I smell the droppings from the mules, the sweat of the men
who drive them. Two boys are playing stickball in the dust of the road.

chapter 4

Artifact and Desire (*Bland, Florida, 1989*)

> Most of the fossils I find are in stream beds or sinks . . . just north
> of here [toward] Bland. This was an old Pleistocene animal bridge.
> We have horses that date back to eighteen million years or so,
> the little three-toed horses that are about the size of a small Collie. . . .
> You have one of the richest Indian heritage areas around.
> —Steve Everett, 1983[1]

My dad's little brother, Willie, like my father, grew up to be a barber. He had a shop in Alachua for sixty years. In the 1930s, at the beginning of the Depression, Uncle Willie married a country girl from Bland, a farming area just northwest of Alachua. Tomye Rivers and my mother became friends and, when I returned to Alachua, Aunt Tomye and I became confidantes. Aunt Tomye supplied something Mother couldn't: she rejoiced in my mere existence. As long as she lived, I could walk in at her back door and be at home. In Aunt Tomye's presence, I was beautiful, brilliant, and had never done wrong.

When I began investigating Bland—only a rudimentary mail stop in 1903 when it was named by its first (and only) postmaster for his young son, Bland Matthews, Aunt Tomye insisted I must meet her sister, Huldah. "This is important," she said, and drove me in her own car to Bland in early 1988 with Uncle Willie, who was quite ill by then, nodding in the back seat behind us. Although as a child I'd been driven by car along CR 241 which passes through Bland, I'd never before traveled its nooks and crannies. I interviewed Huldah, but the interview I'd intended to do with Aunt Tomye was never taped.

On the last day of 1988, the phone rang at my house before 8 a.m. It was a Saturday morning, and the voice that spoke took me completely by surprise: a deputy sheriff told me that my uncle was "incoherent." Could I "come and identify the body of a woman sitting in my aunt's car wearing a blue and white striped housecoat?" That blue and white housecoat was the one Aunt Tomye had bought for her glaucoma surgery.

She had put on her outdoor shoes and started toward the newspaper box at the edge of the highway. When the heart attack began, she must have gotten into the new Ford Taurus to wait it out. Her arms and legs were white and cold; the pores of her skin, tiny blue dots. She wore her wedding rings. Her purse was under her arm with the car keys in it; she sat behind the wheel as though she might crank up and drive off. But her eyes were closed and her mouth slightly open, as though she had been cut off in mid-sentence.

For more than a year, I have tracked an archaeologist's team searching for the lost mission of Santa Fe de Toloca, have watched for months the meticulous movements of their trowels smoothing the inner walls of hundreds of test pits. Now, on a sunny January day, I am on my stomach in a field in Bland, tracing with an index finger along the delicate line between the parietal and temporal plates of a woman's skull. Off a little-traveled country road in north-central Florida, where local folks said all along that evidence of Indian life would be found, a significant discovery is being documented.

Though they may never have heard of the Spanish mission, the people of Bland have for generations had notions about the earlier inhabitants of their farmlands. For more than 150 years, they have been climbing down off their tractors or stopping mules and walking back down furrows to pick up chipped flint objects that shone brightly against the just-turned soil.

Sitting around their hearths at night, men drew out these finds from their pockets and wondered aloud about the people who had left them. On a winter evening as family members sat peeling oranges by the fire, a child's parents might have held out a faceted stone and said, "You see, there's Indians down in them fields. Don't you get off too far from this house." Some of the children remembered the warning and, when they handed down the chipped stone tools to their children, they handed down stories along with them. Confined by logic and the constraints of their science, archaeologists considered the stories of local people "hearsay history," possibilities they would investigate only after other, more objective evidence was considered.

I am propped on one elbow, trying not to put any of my weight near the mouth of this burial site. For months I have stared into squared-off test pits, admired countless vague stains I was told might be evidence of rotted posts

The LeMoyne/DeBry plate of Timucuans working their land. The men are using a type of hoe made of fishbone on a wooden stick, while the women make holes in the soil and drop in the seeds.[2]

that were once building supports, counted hundreds of fluttering pink plastic flags marking the spots where Spanish nails and spikes have been found. I have watched in this silent empty field as the surrounding hickory and maple trees turned yellow and then red, while Ken Johnson's archaeology team sifted sand through mesh, getting their faces and arms more and more deeply tanned. From scraps of corncobs and dried peanut hulls, we can reconstruct a scene of naked toddlers at play beside an outdoor fire where food cooks in a clay pot.

A small sandstorm barely licks the field, whirling fine grit into my mouth and eyes. It is a grit that has been loosened inch by inch from beneath the ground and sifted into high, loose piles in a dedicated and persistent labor with a single aim, described so well by team member Cliff Nelson: "to let the soil fall away from the object."

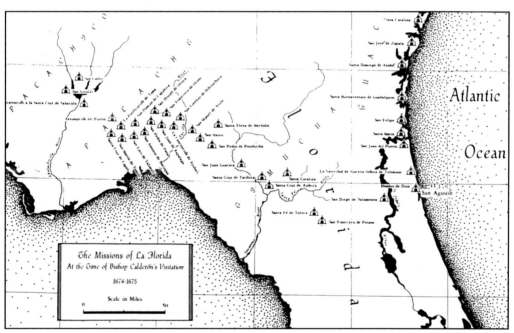

The Missions of La Florida At the Time of Bishop Calderón's Visitation, 1674–1675.[3]

"Object" does not seem the right word for this Potano woman whose skeleton I am contemplating. I cannot see her ribs, which may have dissolved in the 400 years she has lain here. The jointed finger bones are distinguishable on either side of and beneath her chin. During the First Spanish Mission Period (1565–1763), Christianized Indians were buried with their hands crossed over their chests.[4]

The experts are reasonably sure that this is indeed the lost Spanish Mission of Santa Fe de Toloca, where Potanos—one tribe of Timucuan-speaking Indians—were Christianized and trained to work on Spanish cattle ranches. Here, women like this one were convinced to give up moss skirts for more substantial clothing while Spanish priests struggled to change a culture with disconcerting habits such as incestuous marriage for the desired traits of fitness and height. Jacques LeMoyne, writing of Laudonniere's 1564 expedition to Florida, says:

> This Chief Athore was very handsome, wise, honorable, and strong, and at least half a foot taller than the tallest of our men. He was grave and modest, and his bearing was majestic. He had married his own mother and had a number of sons and daughters by her, whom he proudly showed us, striking his thigh as he did so. It is well to remark that after he married his mother, his father, Saturiba, did not live with her any longer.[5]

In Western Europe, young men of Portugal, Spain, England, France, and the Netherlands grew up thinking of expeditions to the New World much as we have thought of the moon since John Glenn's short stunning flight in the spring of 1962. Explorers came to find riches and to convert "the heathen." This connected the Old World to the New and changed forever how men and women looked at the globe. It put ships in the water that brought cattle and horses and peaches and oranges to la Florida, and built the string of missions between St. Augustine and Pensacola that included Santa Fe de Toloca. What remains of the mission lies now many feet below ground, but the shapes of the old buildings, among which the Spanish and Indians ate and prayed together, show in infrared images captured from a NASA plane.

Santa Fe, San Diego, San Francisco, and San Antonio were Florida Spanish-Indian towns 150 years before missions with the same names were established in the western United States. Unlike St. Augustine's Castillo de San Marcos, which still stands, Florida's other Spanish missions have not received much attention. Until the recent appointment of the DeSoto Trail Commission, we have had little schooling in what to look for.

One might look for high elevation near sources of water, for water was not pumped or piped before the Spanish came, but carried in bowls or gourds by hand, and the Spanish, who dug wells, placed missions where they could see for miles around. You can see for a distance of almost fifty miles from high elevations near where the Santa Fe River bridge divides Union and Alachua counties. Young Tomye Rivers, who was born near the river, could see the distant blue hills beyond the next community called Providence as she rode her horse in these woods. Tomye grew up learning how to chop cotton and string tobacco in a farm family that grew everything it ate.

It may be that the acorns the girl Tomye strung into necklaces were descended from the very oak tree whose nuts the Potano woman pounded into gruel for her child. It may be that the Potano woman, too, looked north and marvelled at how far she could see.

When Tomye was a child the sinkholes near where she lived were not yet grown over with vegetation, not yet polluted with chemicals from fertilizers, pesticides, and herbicides spread on the fields. They were swimming holes where, say oldtimers like Mary Lou McFadden, "We would be in there floating on our backs in the heat of the day." In the Potano woman's day, there was not yet run-off from fields of cow manure and the water was clear enough to drink.[6]

While this Potano woman lived, my Aunt Tomye, who died one week ago today, was only a possibility in the genetic code of her great-great-great-great-great grandmother who lived somewhere in Europe and whose descendants would not reach the North American continent for another 150 years.

Tomye's parents, Thomas Jackson Rivers and Ollie Howell Rivers, would not reach Bland until the 1890s, and Tomye would not be born to them until 1910. She would live to see electricity, air flight, carbon dating, and the infrared technology that led to the discovery and opening of this grave. Aunt Tomye would live almost long enough for the arrival of my copy of the Winter 1988 issue of The Georgia Review, which includes an essay by O. B. Hardison, Jr., in which he predicts the creation of a new man, one of silicon rather than carbon: a man who will not die. Hardison says that, someday in the future, we will be able to transfer the best of our humanness to an imperishable body. Hardison says, and he is talking of what computers may make possible for us:

> Silicon man will not need sound to hear music or light to see beauty—
> it was only the need to survive on a dangerous planet sculpted by
> gravity, covered with oxygen and nitrogen, and illuminated by
> a sun, that led carbon creatures to grow feet for walking and ears
> for hearing and eyes for seeing. These are part of the dying animal
> to which carbon man is tied.[7]

If Hardison is right, then someday there may be a way to preserve what we most cherish about being human but, until that time—until we can capture something as wondrous as Aunt Tomye's broad smile in lasting silicon— mourners will continue to stand mutely under canvas canopies listening to ministers summarize the lives of those whose bodies are being committed to the earth. We will continue to cover the fresh-closed graves with floral bouquets worth hundreds of dollars that will quickly wilt and die in the sun. We will continue to examine the artifacts: Tomye's diamond earrings, her *Bible* marked at the Twenty-third Psalm, the sugar from her emptied kitchen cabinet that sweetened the cup of tea I drank this morning, and the scraps of my writing she collected and saved over twenty years.

Until we can replace perishable human beings in a lasting design of silicon or something like it or, as Aunt Tomye might suggest, until we truly penetrate the mysteries of the Twenty-third Psalm, we will continue to wonder at the shared meaning of lives like hers and that of Potano Woman, whose delicate gray skull beneath my hand held memory, thought, hope, and desire. Did she have a child like the one son Tomye adored? Did the approach of that child's father once cause her to tremble in delight?

I can touch her teeth if I like, but I won't. I will not risk loosening the lovely design her long arm bones make crossed under her chin. I slide back from the grave and sit on my heels.

A wind is coming up. Above the line of the hammock at the edge of the field, we will see again tonight a sky pinkened by the deadly chemical soup scientists say is changing our planet.

The crickets start and I stand, thinking an odd thought: that, for tonight, both women lie under the same stars.

chapter 5:

As Far as the River (*Bland, Florida, 1989*)

> We have always been right here on the southern edge of the South.
> They call us the Bible Belt and if there is anything that ties us together
> it is the adoration that Southerners, black and white, have for the
> churches…From the very first settlement at Old Newnansville,
> you will find that the religion and the churches were the unifying
> part of everything that happened.
>
> —Arthur Spencer, Jr., 1983[1]

I love Bland, its hills so high that, when I first saw them, I thought I was being driven into the Smokies, a faraway land I'd only heard of. Bland has two hearts—one black, one white—that beat along the Santa Fe River, in the area called Sugar Hill, at the grave of Potano Woman, and inside the Greater New Hope and New Oak Grove churches encircled by homesteads established 150 years ago.

Driving Bland's dirt roads I recognize the humps in the land that are burial mounds, the streams from which black panthers and aborigines drank. Underneath these plowed fields lie the bones of men, women, and children who arrived in successive migrations (the explorers, colonists, and planters) before early twentieth-century developers carved this state into sweet rectangles and squares and sold them like Hershey bars. Once the Florida panther (*Felis concolor*) and Native American no longer drank in oneness from these streams, Bland's voluptuous hills were regarded as property to be deeded, drained, sliced, and developed—an entire world transformed from the greens and browns of reeds and alligators into columns of figures representing profit and loss.

Nonetheless, here in my favorite section of northwest Alachua County, I still get caught up in what's immediately before me, find another sort of oneness and savor it while I can, as on this Sunday morning when down one aisle—moving as ceremoniously as vestal virgins—come black women all in white and, then, down the other aisle, a long line of men in dark suits marching slowly from the rear of the church to the choir loft in front. The women come down my aisle, their movements synchronized: left-step-pause, right-step-pause. The other aisle is one undulating dark line of men marching in time to Gussie Washington Lee's piano. In an hour, I, too, may want to give my soul to Jesus.

"Take me to the waa-ter. Take me to the waa-ter." A white-kerchiefed, white-robed young girl steps gingerly into the baptismal pool up front. The minister, a muscular black man also robed in white, reaches for her hand.

"Take me to the wa-terr." We are all singing now, choir members and audience, but Gussie's voice rings out loudest, making the microphone in front of her superfluous. This voice must be coming up through an invisible conduit that extends from beneath the piano stool she is sitting on, through the floor, and from underground, out of the deepest part of the earth.

Gussie Lee, lead singer and piano player for the Greater New Hope Missionary Baptist Church, tosses back her black curls and grins at us over her shoulder. We are all on our feet now, shifting in time to the music while Gussie's hands roam the keyboard. She breaks deep bass chords into threes and fingers the highest, tinkly trebles, yet the piano and our voices are mere details in the rich funneling sound that pours out of Gussie's mouth and spreads back over us.

The grandparents of Greater New Hope families farmed these fields 100 years back. Of the people standing with me, few now work the land. Many no longer physically reside in surrounding Bland, but they still call it "home" and every other Sunday is a Homecoming. Dinner "on the grounds" will be served after church but, first, the gradual and inescapable gathering of the black congregation to the ministerial bosom, answering the preacher's pleading questions. Even I, white and a newcomer, feel the building desire for communion. The minister, who refers to himself as "Cunningham," does not actually preach; he has a conversation with the congregation, a "call and response" that goes like this:[2]

"Cunningham say, You don't have to go to the gro-cer-y store… as long as there's food in your house. But if the food…is OUT,… you NEED to GO to Winn Dixie. You needs to go GROCERY SHOPPING! And what I'm saying to you is…is, when you feel yourself getting spiritually low…you need to go to get yourself fed. Satisfied. And there is SAT-IS-FAC-TION…at the foot of the cross. There is as-sur-ance there."

The audience answers, "Yeah, yeah."

"You know what I believe? That when you live right…and the danger DO come…"

"Oh, yeah…"

"You think, well, maybe it's my time…"

"Yeahhh."

"You don't need to run. God said, the day of the Lord will come…"

"Yeahhh," the voices of the people say, and Gussie Lee stretches out her right hand above the keyboard, flexes her fingers.

"What he said on the cross…"

"Yeah."

"Those that are in high places, will run to the mountains and tell the mountains to fall. They'll run to the sea and the sea will dry up. They'll hunt for death, and death will flee them! But he say—the right-eous!…the right-eous…"

"Yeah?"

"Will go…the right-eous…"

"Yeah?"

"Will go away…to eternal life. But the wick-ed, the *Bible* say…"

"Yeah?…"

"…the wicked…"

"Yeah, yeah."

"Will burn forever. But the righteous will go away into eternal life. And live FOR-EV-ERR!"

"Yeahhhhhhh," sighs the audience, throwing scattered handclaps back at Cunningham. Gussie brings down her right hand and recapitulates the preacher's meter in high, tinkly notes.

Cunningham continues: "The only sad part about life is…separation time. When 'mama' will go one way…and the daughter…will go another. I think of when Christ come…and the righteous be caught up with Him…and Mama looking back on her daughter…and Father looking back on his son."

Behind the preacher's words, Gussie pulls a moan out of the bass end of the piano. As Reverend Cunningham paints a verbal mural of parents stretching out their hands toward children disappearing at the edge of the horizon, Gussie turns the sermon into a duet. Immediately before Cunningham pronounces the inevitable judgment, her piano throws out a single, warning chord. Her left foot is constant, keeping the beat. It is just above or hitting the pedal, but her right foot dances, traces circles, hits the floor. It releases; it stabs at the pedal.

"A New Heaven and a New Earth! I see a new heaven and a new earth. When JE-SUS comes."

"Oohh, Je-sus!" breathes Gussie in the voice of a desirous lover, not knowing the microphone has caught her whisper.

Even without music or voices, I would feel the quickening in this congregation. In front of me, an elderly man gets to his feet, swinging into a slow version of movements I last tried while the voice of Fats Domino sang "Blueberry Hill" from a jukebox. The old man swings his arms, throws out one leg. Behind him, a preschool boy in a dress shirt and a bow tie climbs up onto the pew and stands, shaking his small fist.

I am as close as I can get to the Baptist revivals of my childhood and the

sick dread I felt singing, "Just as I am/without one plea" while considering
that perhaps I should walk the aisle. All those many years ago, Grandmother
Strickland stood behind me firmly pressing the heel of her hand hard against my
shoulder in the First Baptist Church of Alachua, urging me forward.

I say I am close to my childhood experience at First Baptist in Alachua, but
actually this feels sweeter, and in a way that has nothing to do with my having
become an adult. Why does this church strike me so differently than those in
town and why am I more comfortable here? The families I've met in Bland—
both black and white—are all evangelical Protestants, either Methodists or
Baptists, as are most townspeople. Yet, here, Christianity seems more of a piece,
the practice of religion more integrated into weekdays as well as Sundays.

Do city commission seats and zoning issues separate country people from
those in town? Would Bland's Washington and Malphurs families somehow be
different if they were transplanted to the city? Farmers sometimes debate over
fence lines and they do compete—for tobacco prices when crops are auctioned,
for example. But could it be that, because they work so intimately with the soil,
they understand better than do their city cousins their true connections?

Bland's families are not crowded together or uniformly separated into city
blocks. Their home places are distinct and individual: I'm told to look for a field
that is hilly or flat, to turn at a gnarled oak or over a cattle gap, and I drive dirt
roads to get there. Does greater space make for spaciousness of heart?

To write about country and city—or even Bland, Traxler, and Santa Fe—as
discrete units is misleading, for they overlap, and the folks who live in one have a
great many things in common with those who live in the other. Still, I wonder if,
waking mornings in the same places their parents and grandparents also yawned
and stretched, these farmers recall in their bones that they are of Bland and
Bland is of them. Perhaps country folk are not misled by arbitrary distinctions
such as section, township, and range. Entwined with river, sky, and vine, like Aunt
Tomye and Potano Woman, they commune all day with those whose stories mark
this place, having hallowed it with generations of toil. Working the land, they are
humbled daily by the cast of the sky and the movement of clouds. The fortunes of

townspeople are calculated differently. They go on buying and selling, regardless of the weather.

Gussie and Cunningham are related to Mary Lou and Vernon not only by a literal geography, but also by a spiritual one; they know they are a part of one another and a part of the earth; they haven't forgotten their common destiny, this lovely dirt to which we all belong.

To the north of Greater New Hope is Sugar Hill, where Gussie Washington's Uncle Lemon was born in 1920. Like many Alachua County residents, Lemon's ancestry becomes a matter of guesswork two generations back. He says:[3]

> I can't recall any relatives that were slaves, but I [did] know a lady out here, Aunt Phoebe Simmons. She was born in slavery. She and her sister was sold at the block, the auction block. I think they was about eighteen years old. Hadn't seen each other since. My mother say the last of the selling of the slaves, [you] take the name of the masters, or 'marsers,' or whatever they call it, and we were Pusos before Washingtons bought us. Freedom was declared [when we were] under the Washingtons. That's where we get our name Washington. That's where all the blacks have got their names. Slavemasters.

With words, Lemon makes his memories vivid. Here are two memories having to do with his father, one at Christmas and one at his death, both told through the eyes of a child:

> It was cold and my daddy had bought me a cap pistol. I liked firecrackers and cap pistols. We couldn't wait 'til daylight: we get up with him, he build a fire before daylight, in the morning. He build a fire in the fireplace, and make a noise like he running Santy Claus out of the

house. And make a dash in the floor like he running [and] say, "Santy Claus going up the chimney!" We hit the floor, no clothes on, no shoes. Get to them stockings! Stockings hanging up before the fireplace . . . . Go out on the porch and holler, and the neighbor would holler back . . . . We was about forty acres apart, every forty acres have a house on it. And they shoot the gun. Something like, Bam! Bam! and they celebrating Merry Christmas morning.

In contrast to his exuberant account of Christmas, Lemon's second story is somber:

Daddy was in the kitchen eating dinner. One Sunday. The sun was shining pretty, and it come up a little shower of rain while the sun was shining, and it lasted about five minutes. Mama came and told us, "Y'all come to the house quick! Your daddy's leaving us." Mr. Arthur Jones made the casket. Made it out of boards, and they would take it and wrap it up in a white sheet so you don't see the wood. You see that white sheet. They carried Papa in the back of a Model-T truck and we followed behind in cars, horse and wagons, and buggies. We stop at the church. They had to let him set out for twenty-four hours cause lot of times people would come back. Not be completely dead, and they'll come back. I was playing with the turkeys as they was coming to get the body and carry it to the cemetery. I was out there making the gobblers strut, and they made us stop playing and be quiet.

Lemon Washington has been farming since he was eight years old. After the burial of their father in Damascus Cemetery, Lemon's big brother Gus put Lemon in the fields where his young boy's view of the world was framed by the high handles of a planter as he guided it behind the shifting buttocks of a mule drawing the planter along as it set tobacco seedlings into the ground. "We be planting tobacco all our lives," Lemon says. "I was driving a tobacco 'slide' [a sort

Lemon Washington in his tobacco field, 1987. Photograph © Barbara B. Gibbs. Used by permission.

Workers stacking cut tobacco, 1987. Photograph © Barbara B. Gibbs. Used by permission.

of sled for transport] when I wasn't tall enough to see across it. Had to look round the edge to see where I was going."

When growers clip the bushy green tops of the tobacco plant to encourage leaf growth, the small tobacco flower is commonly sacrificed. The bloom has a long deep throat that flares into five petals of two lobes each and, in all of Lemon Washington's fields today, there is just one blossom blowing. Beyond the slim yellow line of its stamen and fluted pink petals, three acres of tobacco plants curve in symmetrical rows over the mounded green breast of hill towards the Santa Fe River. At the bottom of the field, a thick line of trees; a gap where water lies but cannot be seen; then, a second line of trees on the river's opposite bank.

This summer day, half a mile from the Santa Fe where he swam as a child, Lemon steers a tractor pulling a shallow trailer alongside lush rows of tobacco. While Lemon drives, four workers move back and forth between the rows and the trailer, harvesting bundles of tobacco leaves. There is no shade in the field and it is so hot that the workers' backs glisten like the black satin of eggplant.

Lemon has confided to me his concerns about future tobacco crops, his worry that he will have to give up curing in old-fashioned barns where fires are hand-stoked. Next year, he may have to invest in expensive metal trailers called "curing barns." Several farmers, including Mary Lou and Vernon, say that tobacco companies are sharing less of their profit with farmers who, after generations on the land, are now sending wives and children to work in town because farming no longer supports their families. They acknowledge the health risks of tobacco use, but (perhaps like antebellum plantation owners who could not imagine survival without their slave economy) they do not happily contemplate the end of family life as they have known it. In an interview with the *Gainesville Sun's* Galen Moses, Bland grower Tommy Malphurs says he doesn't have enough acreage to abandon tobacco and set his sons up to make a living raising row crops and cattle.

I watched my father die of emphysema, so I am not about to mount an argument in favor of cigarettes. Nevertheless, people like Malphurs are feeling more than nostalgia. They are part of a "cultural lag" in which the culture has changed its mind about their product, and they are left behind.[4]

Lemon Washington, who is also a preacher, confronts the possibility of being left behind from a faith perspective. In spite of his father's early death and heavy family responsibilities, Washington describes himself as having grown up to be "a pretty good devil." As he tells of his youth, his eyes dance behind the shining rims of his glasses and his delight in mischief is easy to imagine.

Lemon says that, "For seven whole years, before I gave up my girls, and my liquor, and my fun," again and again he heard God say, "Gone make you preach." Lemon had traditionally spent his Sunday mornings "cutting donuts in the church parking lot." The news that he would preach was treated as a joke by everyone who knew him, right up until he opened his *Bible* to Isaiah 40: 7-8 and began:

> The grass withereth, the flower fadeth: because the spirit
> of the Lord bloweth upon it; Surely the people is grass.
> The grass withereth, the flower fadeth; but the word of
> our God shall stand forever.[5]

Lemon has preached the last thirty of his fifty-eight years and, in spite of the heat of fields and tobacco barns, and the possible elimination of the tobacco warehouse auction system (to be replaced by a "before harvest" agreement between large tobacco companies and individual farmers), his taped interview with me is a perfect balance of faith and humor. He slaps his leg and tells how, before his conversion, he drove about blowing a three-toned trumpet attached to his car horn. "Cut right across wire fences," he says. "Go through the fields! Crazy!" When he laughs, the gold fillings in his teeth glitter.

Two weeks after I tour Lemon's fields, on a sweltering August morning the New Big Dollar Tobacco Market opens in High Springs with dozens of men already standing in line behind auctioneer Matt Dykes and his co-owner, Tommy Malphurs. "Seventy-seventy-seventy-five," Dykes begins, gesturing toward the thousands of yellow bales on the blue floor of the warehouse where the thermometer registers 110 degrees.

Dykes is a big jowly man whose stomach protrudes over his red pants and whose face wears a sour look. He proceeds, punctuating calls with curse words. "Eighty-dollar, hundred-eighty." Wriggling through the rows of tobacco like a polyester centipede, the line of buyers behind Dykes starts to move, their faces even sterner than his. Two buyers step aside, allowing others to pass. The remaining segments of the centipede march on. The most serious man in the group sets his lips in a grim line and never falls out of step. He reaches into the middle of each bale he passes, pulling leaves from its center, scattering them onto the floor. Finally, he steps out of his place and onto the bales, walking an entire row, setting his feet carefully down into their centers, one bundle at a time.

Two growers stand against the wall, watching. One says to the other, "A house full of dang sure pretty tobacco, but [buyers] just put in not to buy no tobacco today." True, they are not buying, possibly because supervisors (called "circuit riders") are in evidence. Buyers are said to bid more generously on the days their bosses are not present.

"These government graders ain't got no heart," someone mutters. Then a young man called Johnny jumps up, runs along behind the line of buyers, bends over the line of tobacco, and tears off the price tags affixed moments ago by the auctioneer. Johnny looks back at the other growers and calls out, "I got nine months in this already. If I'm gone go in the hole, I'll go in next week." Johnny means to reclaim his tobacco and hold it until the next auction day. A single crop requires a nine-month growing period.

"Set seed beds in December, you don't finish until September, and [then] you just never know," says Gerald Emerson, whose family has been growing tobacco in Bland for four generations. "My daddy said he's been growing tobacco for fifty-seven years and still don't know a thing about it."

Over Gerald's shoulder, I see Johnny's profile. Nearly finished ripping the price tags off his year's work, he stands back from the last fat bale. As he stares down at the tobacco, a drop of water forms at the tip of his nose and hangs there a moment, then falls.

After the sale, I interview New Big Dollar co-owner, Tommy Malphurs, who, it turns out, is my cousin by marriage; he's Huldah's son and was named by Aunt Tomye (a young girl when Tommy was born) for herself. My family's connections have given me access no stranger could achieve. "Oh!" people say, "You're Allen's girl." Tommy tells me he played end for the Alachua Indians high school football team in the early 1940s, when I was too young to remember, but my being Tomye Cauthen's niece connects us.

Before we are done discussing the tobacco market, I learn that Tommy Malphurs is also an expert hunter. My father shot some birds once, down in our back field, and I remember one occasion when there was rabbit on the table, but Daddy never really cared for hunting. Uncle Willie's avocation is coon hunting and he has some dogs. This is a part of my cultural heritage I know almost nothing about, so I get myself invited to go fox hunting.

I meet Tommy at 11 p.m. on a Saturday night in late October in a Kwik-Stop parking lot in High Springs, and we head north in his pickup to join his son and a friend named Henry. I expect that we will be running through the woods all night and have removed my earrings. I wear cowboy boots and a red jacket, but fox hunting turns out to be nothing like what I expected.

While we drive, a high keening sounds from the cages in the truck bed as though the dogs are in pain, or badly want something they cannot have. The closer the truck gets to Lafayette County and the hunting pen, the higher and more pained the canine music becomes.

"Why are they doing that?" I ask, meaning also the fierce beating of their tails against the sides of the truck.

"Been here before," says Tommy, parking in front of a high metal fence gate and getting out. The dogs howl wildly, as though this is their last night on Earth. As Tommy approaches with keys jangling, they wedge their muzzles between the iron bars of their cages.

Two dozen medium-sized brown and white Walker hounds scramble from the truck. Identical copies of one another, they run off into the dark, noses to the ground, sniffing out some delicacy. As soon as they disappear, we settle in around the fire.

Tommy chucks broken pieces of tree limbs into a barrel and flames flare. Late October in North Florida is merely jacket-cold; the fire in the barrel provides a focal point. For a moment, I imagine the glowing barrel's real function is to mark where we are. In the great, dark county of Lafayette, on a peninsula called Florida, at the tip of the North American continent, our light is insignificant.

We are small—dogs, men, the fenced-in foxes, and me—on a planet orbiting the sun at a speed of eighteen and one-half miles per second. We take for granted a sun that persists in predictably hurling itself around its galaxy, and spectacles like the Orionid meteor shower two nights ago. Above the horizon at four degrees north, the moon, Venus, and Mars glimmer.

"That sounds like Low Ball, don't it?" Tommy leans his heavy frame out of a portable lawn chair and towards the fire. "Hey, Henry! Don't that sound like Low Ball?"

Tommy's friend, Henry Sims, cocks his head toward the distant braying of one dog's voice that sings out louder than all the rest. Sims, like Tommy, has driven a pickup truck full of dogs for more than an hour to get here from his home. Now Sims looks up at the sky, pulls his jacket closed, and shakes his head. "Naw," he says, "That ain't Low Ball. I believe that's Richard."

All the way here in the truck, Tommy talked dogs. He does more than run them through fields; he also breeds and shows them and, more than a dozen times, has mastered and judged United States Open Field Trials. He tells me that some breeders are so serious about their dogs' gene pools that, when they get "ugly puppies," they destroy the entire litter. A family called Walker breeds these hounds "from the granddaddy called 'Tennessee Lee.'" Tommy says that, for speed and tracking, Walker hounds are the best.

"It's in the breeding. A pit bull, for instance. You take a bulldog, he wants to catch. Fight."

"Isn't that fighting illegal?" I ask.

"I've never known it to be legal," Tommy chuckles. "But used to be a good bit of it over there up around Lake City and over around Starke. There's a man, filthiest old fellow you ever looked at in your life and, at one time, they said he had rattlesnakes in his bathtub. He's got a house you'd swear nobody lived there, and he's got the front door boarded up, nailed across like a barn. And he's got seventy-five or a hundred pit bulls. Ties 'em up individually, where they can't get together."

"Why can't they be together?"

"He's got bulldogs over there that's so bad to fight that they can't even put a female in to breed. They just got to back 'em up at the door of the pen for the dog to breed her."

"That's mean," I offer.

"That's the kind they want. So your dog can kill my dog. Not me, though. I hate a dogfight and I've never been to one. But some of my friends fought dogs and they say they'll chew their legs off and that pit bull will still be crawling up there on his belly…without any legs. Still fighting."

"This hunting goes way back," Tommy adds. "George Washington was a fox hunter. The British. Redcoats. This sport belonged to kings."

We sit around the fire, mostly silent. Tommy and Henry do the talking. They have known each other for thirty years and some of their dogs are related. The two men have been hunting together for a long time. Tonight, they each paid $100 to rent this 300-acre "pen" with a high fence; the enclosure is topped with a lip like those around prison yards and an electric wire is buried a foot underground.

Tommy and Henry talk of their own pen, the one they are going to build for themselves and then charge others to use. "Make back our investment," they say. They will import coyote and fox. The animals cost as much as $100 each, so they must be kept wormed and healthy. And fed.

During a long hour of silence, I decide the others must be asleep. Then, in the dark, Tommy says, "Tony wasn't worth the hind leg offa Mark." No answer from Sims. In the quiet that follows, a star streaks across the sky and I remind myself that Tony and Mark are dogs. All night, the Little Dipper follows the Big Dipper, extending the long rhinestone arm of its handle toward the west.

When I have counted dozens of falling stars, more than in all my life before put together, a frenzied yelping begins—in the far corner of the pen, the men say. "They've found 'em a fox," they announce.

Against the distant curtain of barking, Malphurs and Sims talk:

"That ain't Richard."

"That's 151."

"No, it ain't. That ain't Richard."

"*That* is Richard."

I strain to make out the dogs' individual voices, to discriminate as the men do, and fail. I return to examining the melted crystal strands in the sky, knowing I am looking at just one arm in the Milky Way. If it were possible to situate myself at some other point in space, gaining a different perspective, I might be able to locate our foxhunting pen in this galaxy containing Earth, Sun, and solar system.

In the dark, shapes of dogs appear, jump into the back of the truck, and lie down. They have prematurely quit.

"That one ain't got no excuse except sorriness," Tommy complains, turning his flashlight beam toward the truck. The first guilty dog blinks his eyes and puts his head down between his paws.

"That old Susy, bitch," says Sims.

Before daylight, several more of the dogs bred at such cost for running and tracking have quit. Some, recently back from the state trials, we recognize by their three-digit fluorescent numbers that appear at the edge of the road, then leap noiselessly into the truck.

"Low Ball and Number 151 was coming down the road and they wasn't even in the race," reports Tommy, with disgust. He has been to the far side of the pen and back to discover which dogs are not performing. "Some of them not worth two whoops in torment," he adds.

The one cricket that chirped all night hushes, and a tree's limbs take shape against a black sky turning silver. Like a reflection on water, the tree's foliage quivers against the coming light. But this clear pool of silver is sky and, between that sky pool and me, the last strands of orange fire waver above the barrel. We have consumed packages of weiners skewered on short lengths of pecan limbs and cooked over the barrel of fire, nearly four bags of Oreo cookies, and steadily drunk Coca-Colas to keep us awake. The constellations are all at my back, half the expensive dogs in a pile at the rear of the truck.

We gather blankets, fold chairs, stuff weiners and Oreos back into wrappers that have lain open all night on the hood of Tommy's truck. I ask a question about Tommy's mother: "What does Huldah think about your hunting?"

"She said I was crazy, I run it in the dirt, I done too much of it, I got too many dogs, and all that. And I tease her. When I was born, she had an old Buick automobile, and it was big enough that they could take the back seat off and put a kiddy koop in the back, mostly when they was gonna have a supper or a picnic. But she'd put a kiddy koop in the back of the car and put me in it [and take me hunting]. So I told her, I said, 'Mother, you trained me, you started me.' They say, 'When you start out carrying 'em about like that, you see what happens.'"

"How can you love dogs so much?"

"Bred in me," he says. "Daddy run dogs. I run dogs."

I shake my head, laugh, and climb up into the truck. Tommy drives slowly up and down between cornrows, looking for dogs that are still out. Squinting down one long furrow, I see the morning's first ray of sunlight enter Lafayette County, illuminating the soil between two rows of parched corn. Yesterday, a friend attempting to explain to me astronomy's black holes used the term "event horizon," the point—my friend said—beyond which we can no longer get information. I figure I am there, and fall asleep sitting upright in the truck.

A summer Sunday morning, and I am driving through Bland and north-northwest toward the Sanchez Grant, away from the hills rounding out of the river country that Gussie and Lemon call home.[6] In Gussie's childhood memory, her father sits back on his heels, sifts purple dirt from hand to hand, and proclaims over and over again, "This is such good soil."

I am driving a silent, timeless road, on my way to Huldah Malphurs's house while the doves make soft, thudding sounds against the window of morning. Light falls through the tall trees and thick, curving stands of kudzu, throwing soft splotches on the land. Here is Letha's locust tree, leaning out full of pods, its pink flowers gone. The pods dangle in bunches, their flatness broken by elliptical seeds bulging beneath transparent skins, turning from green to brown.

Stiff-legged white cowbirds stalk up and down in a newly mown field, though there are no cows in sight. The Spanish, who brought our continent's first cattle, have been romanticized, their march through these woods attributed to a wild passion for *la Florida*. But they could never have loved her like the sisters Mary Lou and Vernon McFadden, in whose stories passion measures itself out in small increments of clearing, digging, sweating, hunger, and disease, whose idea of a fitting end is to die "right on the land."

Love changes one's vision and, as I drive, mine is so keen I see a thing normally unnoticed: a hairlike emerald green vine, its red flowers smaller than the smallest of my fingernails, has woven itself into a cover for a telephone cable box. Chinaberry trees grow in the fencerows and the pouting, orange lips of trumpet creeper hang from barbed wire fences. It is early yet but, in an hour, people on their way to church will drive busily past the kudzu covered with limestone dust and a solemn dog, powdered white with the dust, who sits on his hindquarters at the edge of the road.

I pass the pens of dogs in Tommy's front yard and turn into his mother's driveway that angles off under green hickories towards the gabled red house that holds so many lives, so many stories. I pull up under the enormous limbs of a pecan tree that was here in 1928, when Huldah married York Malphurs and came to live with him in his parents' home. Huldah says, "My father-in-law had brought home three nuts in his pocket one day and Mother Malphurs planted all three. Two came up and then something broke one down. Last year I sold close to $500 worth off that one tree."

Beyond the end of the drive, in Huldah's cow pen, are more of Tommy's dogs, their faces circles in the saffron haze of morning light suffering through the vines and grasses dying on the pen's floor. I am here to help bake unleavened bread for communion at Huldah's New Oak Grove Baptist Church.

When Huldah takes the bread out of the oven, it is piecrust crisp and done, but not brown. It is made with flour, water, and "just a tiny bit of oil in it to keep it from being so tough you can't chew it up," she says. Heat radiates from the metal pan as Huldah rocks a knife blade from tip to heel, scoring the flat bread so it can be broken into more than 100 marble-sized pieces. "My grandyounguns likes this," she tells me. "I told 'em, I'll make a whole batch of this stuff some time and let you eat all you want of it. I don't know why it is, but they like it." Since her mother-in-law died forty years ago, the communion preparations at the church have been Huldah's task.[7]

Huldah's silver serving tray has indentations for thimble-sized communion cups and a lid topped with a silver cross. A forty-ounce bottle of Thrifty Maid grape juice from the Monterey Canning Company in San Mateo, California, sits on the table with several thin cups. "Those heavy ones with the thick lips, they have been here about sixty, sixty-five years. Just shows how much more material was used then, what we once got for our money compared to now."

Huldah shows me a special bottle with an atomizer that she uses to fill the cups. "It measures out a tiny bit with each squeeze. You squeeze this little rubber bulb and it draws up through this silver, metal-colored stem. Just a tiny bit of the grape juice." Huldah pulls the long metal straw from the bottle and puts it back into a cardboard carton labeled "Worship Aids."

Minute, lace-like stitches hem the folded, white cloths on the table. The fabric is nubby, like fine writing paper. "Irish linen," Huldah says, "but you can't keep 'em from wrinkling. They've got these cloths in Perma-Prest now."

The small lumps of bread will be served on two-tiered serving dishes stamped "Broadman Press, Nashville." I ask, "Those grandchildren won't come in and eat this stuff up before you leave for church, will they?"

Huldah, a Sunday School teacher and lover of scripture, laughs. "There was a family man, and his wife and two children came into our church. The little boy and little girl were about eight or ten and they were just watching everything in the communion service. Of course, they couldn't partake of it, and I knew they were curious. I left the things up there after the service that night, and the next day I went to bring it home. That family lived right beyond the church, so I took some, just like it was. There was a little bit of juice left in some of the cups and a little bit of the bread. I asked the mother and father if they minded me explaining to those children about communion, and giving them a piece of the bread and a drink from the cups."

"How did you explain it to them?"

"I told them that, when Our Lord died on the cross, He made this ordinance, the Last Supper. I tried to explain the Last Supper to them, about the bread and likening it to His body and the juice to His blood that He was sacrificing on the cross for us. And as often as we did that, we did it in remembrance of Him. Some parents wouldn't let you do a thing like that. You know, if you run up with a Catholic or somebody else, they'd want to shoot you." [8]

It is nearly time to leave for church, and I ask what scripture she studied for today. "It's Exodus, the nineteenth and twentieth chapters," she says. "It's about meeting God in various ways. You know, the mystery and all, and the covenant."

I leave Huldah's house and drive toward the Bellamy Road. On the roadside, the throats of white, fluted morning glories are fading into pink. The small fleabane blossoms have centers as yellow as suns. I drive slowly, counting the individual barbs on a wire fence.

At the far end of the pasture in front of me, a pure white horse switches his tail, draws all the sunshine in the field toward him, then whips his tail forward. A glistening line of light moves along his spine from rump to curve of neck to where his head connects with the ground.

I am already thinking about tomorrow at Lemon Washington's house: I imagine black and white kittens dozing in the heat beneath the wrinkled flowers of a pink crape myrtle tree while a dozen women work in pairs, stringing tobacco

Janie Washington stringing tobacco, 1987.
Photograph © Barbara B. Gibbs. Used by permission.

under a small shed. Lemon's wife, Jamie Washington, lifts tobacco from a big pile, bunches it together, hands it to the person behind, reaches back to the pile, and gathers another bunch by its stems; all this in one seamless motion called "handing."

A second woman wraps string about the bunch of stems handed to her, twists with a practiced weaving movement, then reaches for another bunch, continuing until thirty-five bunches of tobacco are fastened to one long stick. The filled stick is lifted out, and another set into the frame that holds the sticks in place for curing over hand-stoked fires.

Six pairs of women are "handing" and "stringing," their fingers sticky with tar from the leaves, rivulets of sweat rolling down their faces. This scene at Lemon's, like Tommy's dogs and Huldah's baking, is a part of Bland, the part which still knows its ancient connections to Earth.

Across these fields at Huldah's New Oak Grove Baptist Church, men, women, and children will soon be lifting those tiny cups. One at a time, they will take the cups into their hands and hold them, their minds intent on the words of Christ being repeated by the minister: "Do this in remembrance of me."

The people lift their cups, and while they are swallowing the bloodied red juice of the grape, Gussie Lee, in her church less than a mile away, feels a wet trickle of sweat that starts from her hairline. The line of moisture curves down her face to the angle of her jaw, then drips while her song finishes rising out of her throat. Gussie hits the keys of the piano and throws back her head, the sound pouring from her mouth all liquid power measured out in one long, fluid caress that lengthens, widens, and settles over Lemon's harvested tobacco, the saffroned dog pen, this land as far as the river.

PART TWO:

THE TOWN

Reminiscent of my Strickland grandparents' front entrance is this swing on the dilapidated porch of former postmaster Clara Gay's home, 1988. This scene is typical for the area prior to air conditioning when, in summer, whole families waited on their porches until the lower temperatures of the night air cooled their homes' interiors and they could go in to bed. Photograph © Barbara B. Gibbs. Used by permission.

At Home, Estranged (*Oxford, Mississippi, 1990*)

> Your father found a bigger place out by Monteocha, at Cooter Pond.
> "Wait a minute," I said to Allen. "I'm as far out in the country as
> I want to go."
>
> —Hortense Cauthen, 1983[1]

I first felt the town's indelible weight through Mama's Victorian interpretations. She had grown up in the town and, according to her, its people were alert to our every move. Even on the farm, we felt their eyes. I escaped them by riding my horse to the back of the field and climbing my favorite tree, a Chinaberry in whose forked branches I sat for hours, reading. I couldn't hear Mama even when she yelled, though sometimes, if I looked up and saw a small figure waving vigorously from the back fence, I came on home.

For years after I returned to live in Alachua as an adult, I collected my mail from the post office after dark, took my exercise walks at night, alone, and never used my front door which could be seen from the street. I wanted to avoid the townspeople; I didn't want them to see me. "At home, estranged," a visiting friend proclaimed.

By Mama's lights, Alachua was a living courtroom in which she was always on trial. If you listened to her, we all were. I was forty and she was still monitoring me, now, about accepting an invitation to swim in a private pool:

"I wouldn't be going out there to their house every day if I was you."

"What do you mean?"

"I mean, I wouldn't be doing it."

"Doing what?"

"Going out to their place every day and swimming in their pool. It just doesn't look right."

"But, Mama, they invited me to use the pool."

"Well, I sure wouldn't. Somebody will have something to say about it."

Mother was concerned with form and, if she were telling this, she'd go about it differently. She'd think first of how it looks. When she organized our family photo album, on the left side of the first page she put a picture of herself wearing a navy skirt, dressy white blouse, and high-heeled shoes and, opposite her, one of Daddy dressed all in white—shoes, shirts, slacks—the works. Daddy's holding a white hat and his hair is black. Mama's was completely white, even before they married. Slightly below the narrow space between those first two pictures, she pasted one of the farmhouse they moved into before I was born. Then me, a baby hugging a soft doll, lying on a pallet in the sunshine in front of a weathered cypress wall. Behind the house's pitched tin roof, a mule angles his head over the barnyard fence and into the picture.

Mother left out her first child, who died at birth: "Little Brother." Somewhere, I once saw a picture taken at Antioch Cemetery of my father, glassy-eyed, holding the small bundle that was his infant son's blanket-wrapped body. At the gravesite, Daddy insisted on undressing the baby. Looking for some visible reason for his boy's death, Aunt Nadine said. Daddy thought it was punishment for all his drinking.

Until I was a teenager and visited a girlfriend who lived in town, I knew only three places there: my grandparents' Queen Anne house, the First Baptist Church, and the school. I saw them first through my mother's eyes. She had grown up in the house to which she had one of her first graders deliver me, a preschooler, on weekday mornings while she was opening class at the same Alachua school she'd attended as a child. She was the first person baptized in our yellow brick

Sudye with her parents, Allen and Hortense Cauthen, 1946.
Here, mother is pregnant with my sister, Emily. From a family album.
Used by permission.

church, built in 1918. She knew these places as well as her own face in the bathroom mirror.

When I entered kindergarten, I was allowed to walk alone the short dirt lane to Grandmother's. She had bought the house with Granddaddy Meggs's life insurance money, moved Mother, Aunt Nancy, and Uncle Colson in, and advertised it as a boardinghouse. But people didn't have to sleep there to eat her chicken and dumplings, hoecakes, and fried fish; they could come just for lunch. One night, Mother, wakeful in her front bedroom, overheard the parlor ceremony in which Grandmother married one of her boarders, Malachi Strickland.

The family had been Methodist until Grandmother remarried. Now, they attended the First Baptist Church where Granddaddy Strickland was a founding member and a deacon. He took his duties seriously, operating the house as nearly as possible like an outpost of First Baptist. Most of my conversations with him were biblically based and today, considering my grandparents and their influence, I realize that, as a child, I saw little more in them than the rigidity of the couple in Grant Wood's painting, *American Gothic*.

Among my grandparents' dearest friends were the three Morgans, retired missionaries who came each winter to visit and stayed for several weeks. When we heard acorns crunching under car wheels, we ran to the kitchen window and watched as Dr. Morgan slowly pulled his car and house trailer into the dirt lane, then parked under the limbs of a big oak near the back door. Wearing voile dresses and lace-up shoes, Mrs. Morgan and her grown-up daughter Constance jumped out with brooms and swept up the crushed acorns. Then they set up folding chairs and had a cold supper laid by the time Dr. Morgan got the trailer's electric and water lines hooked up. After supper, they were ready to give lessons.

In between *Bible* verses and songs, the Morgans told us stories about the Chinese heathen they had converted and saved from Hell. Constance handed out colored paper, scissors, and paste for the construction of one-inch-square gospel books. As my sister and I dutifully cut and pasted together inch-square bits of paper, Constance sang the story symbolized by each double-spread page: red for my scarlet sins, black for Hell, yellow for God's love, blue and green for the sky my scarlet sins, black for Hell, yellow for God's love, blue and green for the sky and the earth He had created, and white for my soul after Jesus washed it clean. The books had no words. Subsequent lessons began with our singing this song for Constance as each week we cut and pasted new books. We were to carry the books with us at all times but, inevitably, mine got lost in the corners of my pockets and came out of my washed clothes as pea-shaped balls of lint.

Though we may have thought a little less fervently about our salvation, we were more relaxed when the Morgans left because, for one thing, Grandmother could go back to cooking in the aluminum pots they had warned her against. Even without their influence, however, the Strickland house remained orderly, governed by Granddaddy's rules. Daily, he read the *Southern Baptist Handbook*, along with his *Bible* readings, after lunch. In good weather, he read lying in the front porch swing and, afterwards, fell asleep there.

A family portrait on the front steps of the Strickland house, Alachua, c. 1957. Back row (left to right): Sudye Cauthen, Nancy Meggs McWhinnie, and Emily Cauthen; front row (left to right): Malachi Strickland, Willie Colson (Meggs) Strickland, Hortense Meggs Cauthen, and Allen Goolsby Cauthen. From a family album. Used by permission.

The front porch was off the parlor which was cool, dark, and quiet, and, when I was a child, never used. No one played the piano or read the musty books Uncle Colson left stored in the oak secretary when he went away to World War II, and wherever he lived after that. Except me. I read the books and I also played the upright piano, though I was often made to stop because Granddaddy was napping (a perplexing reason, since he was deaf). While he slept, I took off my shoes and silently leapt from one piece of furniture to another, admiring my image in Grandmother's gold-framed mirror which hung over the fireplace from a heavy cord and reflected the entire room.

Grandmother's ruby red wool rug was her most exotic possession. Its patterned intricacies and elaborate scrolled borders made it a magic carpet. On it, I followed Uncle Colson to sea and watched while an artist tattooed the blue anchors that flexed on his biceps when he lifted me above his head. I didn't see him often. He was the family's mystery man, an especially interesting one whose world I had entered through the glorious pictures of his travel books and through the heads of characters unlike anyone I knew, in stories like *God's Little Acre*.

No food or coffee ever appeared on the parlor's glass-topped coffee table. It held only a silver miniature of St. Peter's Cathedral sent by Aunt Nancy who had gone to New York City to get trained as a nurse after St. Luke's in Jacksonville said she was too fat. She had no children and Uncle Colson and his children were never around. There were hundreds of faded, oval pictures of relatives in the velvet album that sat on a special stand beside the old clock in the living room, but I had no cousins to play with. There was my younger sister, but I recall her in the parlor only once, the day she threw a wedge of wood used as a doorstop and cut my face. I still have the scar.

Aunt Nancy could see the Empire State Building from her Manhattan apartment window and she had married a sea captain, a Scot who came to America as an apprentice to Edward J. Smith, the captain who later went down with his ship, the *Titanic*. Aunt Nancy sent us bracelets from Queen Elizabeth's coronation, red plaid taffeta dresses, and woven caps from Fair Isle off the coast of Scotland. She sent me what I thought was the most beautiful doll in the world, a wooden one with painted-on hair and eyes that opened and closed—until my sister decapitated her.

I lay on the high-backed sofa under a window that looked out on the porch where Granddaddy was sleeping and pictured myself somewhere else, somewhere far away, floating on my back in the China Sea, perhaps—its perimeters bordered with the blue and white pattern of my mother's willowware plates—watching the mandarin's daughter and her lover as they turned into birds and flew to the horizon. Aunt Nancy and Uncle Colson had got far away from Alachua, from where I lay rubbing my hand along the glossy fabric of the horsehair sofa, looking up at my small length in Grandmother's mantel mirror, imagining myself in the China Sea under a faultless sun.

Colsen H. Meggs (Uncle Colson) with his young bride, Carolyn Kahlich, of High Springs, shortly before the birth of their first child in 1927. From a family album. Used by permission.

This was before television or the beginnings of rock-and-roll, and it was a quiet house, even when Granddaddy was not napping. Again and again, on an old Victrola in the front room I played Victor Herbert's recording, "March of the Wooden Soldiers," from *Babes in Toyland*. Sometimes I got bored and ventured out on the porch.

"Can't be real chains in Hell, Granddaddy."

Granddaddy looked up from his reading, hit the dial on his hearing aid with one finger, and cocked his head.

"Can't be real fires, either."

"And he opened the bottomless pit; and there arose a smoke out of the pit, as the smoke of a great furnace; and the sun and the air were darkened by reason of the smoke of the pit."

He stared at me like there was nothing more to say.

"Granddaddy, that must mean it would only seem to be like a real fire and seem like chains. Fire hot as you say would melt those old chains right off."

Granddaddy was named for Malachi, the last Old Testament prophet, and Mother said he took the *Bible* literally, confiding to her his belief that the Lord's Supper the Baptists celebrated with saltine crackers and bitter grape juice four times a year was the actual Body of Christ. I doubt Granddaddy realized he had embraced Roman Catholic doctrine. And the Baptists at church never found out; if they had, they wouldn't fondly remember him as "Uncle Mallie."

Although I heard stories, songs, and sermons about God's love, I was mostly occupied with avoiding his displeasure: not using one's talents was one of the sins I was taught about in Sunday School. I'd ask God's forgiveness whenever I hadn't written anything for whole weeks. I memorized scripture, sang in the choir, put coins in the collection plate. No one knew that in my prayers I bargained, asking Him not to take away the words that hummed in my head, marveling that each time I came back to it, writing was still there—as dependable a thing as I had found in this world.

I attended Vacation Bible School, marching through the still cool air of the early summer mornings, up the high church steps with the other children, beneath the bell pull that hung just above our heads in the vestibule, and down the aisle splotched with the greens and golds of the stained glass windows. I loved the tinkling piano we marched to, and the American and Christian flags we saluted. I meant it when I saluted the *Bible* and pledged, "Let the words of my mouth and the meditations of my heart be acceptable to you, O Lord, my strength and my redeemer."

In my preschool Sunbeams group, I learned to recite from the Gospel according to St. John and, when I became a teenager and a member of the Girls' Auxiliary (G.A.), completed the "Maiden," "Lady-in-Waiting," "Princess," and "Queen" steps, after which, robed in white, I was "crowned" in a ceremony in Gainesville.

The requirements for becoming a G.A. Queen included memorizing the names and addresses of all Southern Baptist missionaries. There were hundreds and, as I finished up the last of them sitting in a hot car waiting for my mother to come from a faculty meeting, I promised myself I would never again memorize anything.

Mama taught Sunday School as well as Vacation Bible School and also recruited an "angel choir" of preschoolers who wore pale pink robes with white bows that tied under their chins. While Mother directed, I accompanied them on the piano.

She was not dour, my mother, just nervous and terribly self-conscious. As a young woman, she had sung in the church choir. One Sunday when she stood up to sing, the plain slip she wore under her dress fell to her ankles and bunched up over her shoes. Telling this, she laughed, "Just folded it up and put it in my purse." She had momentary flashes of irreverence, like the time we were singing, "Will There Be Any Stars in My Crown?," when she chuckled and whispered into my ear, "I just hope they'll let me in." An old photograph from Mother's flapper days shows her in the rumble seat of a Ford roadster, standing on her head with her legs up in the air. Clearly, Mother had been less restrained before her marriage.

In church, I was moved by emotion, but I didn't grasp why we must "die for

Jesus." Like Granddaddy, I inclined toward literalism. I made friends with a succession of ministers' children and then lamented when the deacons, for reasons discussed only in closed meetings, sent those families away. I was dismissed by a Sunday School teacher who would not let me explain that, regardless of any burning bush, the Ten Commandments were plain common sense.

The Baptists were not long on logic, but they reached me with their music. Most of all, I loved the songs of a revivalist named Don, a handsome man with shiny black hair who had found Jesus in prison and, when he was released, took to the highways to tell his story in song:

> Ju-ust a clo-ser walk with Theee.
> Grant it, Je-sus, is my plee-ee
> I'llllllll be sat-is-fied as loo-ong
> as I walk, let me walk close to Thee.

Don crooned and the choir hummed, pulling at me like a magnet. I longed to go forward, but I had already been baptized. I wished I had waited for Don.

At home, riding my horse, I explored the most remote fields of our farm which joined San Felasco Hammock, where I liked to imagine panthers and Indians still roamed. I preferred the country to the city, but even in the town I was able to discover a way into mystery: a secret stairway so narrow my shoulders rubbed its musty walls as I climbed stealthily up from the church basement to a small door which opened onto a filled baptistery tank. The same stained-glass Jesus I had watched from a pew out front during baptisms was tending his sheep above the tank's darkened back wall. I had already been immersed by the preacher but, as I stood alone there, the tank looked perilously deep. Near my foot hung a frail ladder of three steps. When the heavy velvet hanging at the front of the tank moved, I jumped; air blowing up from the basement stairs, I supposed.

I shivered and hugged myself. Then I remembered that, after all, I could swim. I was a good swimmer, even though I had almost drowned once, when, for an unending moment underwater, I had groped toward the blurred shapes of my fellow swimming students. There in the gloomy baptistery, standing alone above the vastness of the tank, I reassured myself that I was not afraid. I knew how freeing it could be to lean back and let the water take you.

I hated school: I was the smallest, youngest student and my regular preschool playmate, Ronnie Chambers (who lived on the farm nearest ours), had found himself a new girlfriend in kindergarten. When the teacher privately polled us for Homecoming Court nominees, I fingered the tiny Red Cross pin on my collar and said that I wanted to be in the court. I voted for myself and Ronnie, and I was hurt when he and his new girlfriend won.[2]

If I hated kindergarten, I detested first grade. Although there were two sections, I was put in Mother's, only she wasn't my mother any more. She let me know at once that, at school, she was Teacher. I spent the entire year sending her messages coded with our cat's name, the horse's name, Daddy's name; anything to get her to recognize me as her daughter. But she was determined not to be criticized for favoritism and when I "acted up" she would call me to the front of the room, get out her wooden ruler, and turn me over her knee while my classmates watched.

Mama had a wide, heavy desk at the front of the room and a small American flag that fit like a peg into a hole on the desktop. There were easels, blackboards, and a piano on which Mama exuberantly banged out chords while we sang

> Camels and Bears
> and ponies are found
> prancing around
> on the merry-go-round.
> Toodle-ee-o, toodle-ee-o,
> come take a ride
> there's a pony for you.

My mother was a dedicated teacher. She brought milk we shook into butter, waffle irons, and maple syrup she poured onto the waffles we made. Our Valentine's Day box was large and red, covered with white paper doilies, and it had a slit on top where we dropped in the valentines. Our large airy room had ceiling-high windows on one wall and a cloakroom on the other. I sometimes lingered in the cloakroom, touching the other children's coats, rubbing the fabrics, imagining their warmth. When my classmates lined up after lunch to march out of the cafeteria and across the playground, through the auditorium, and down the long wooden hallway to Mother's room, I raced ahead to steal a few minutes with Mrs. Trinkner.

Marion Trinkner taught in a sunlit classroom with a special rug that was divided into squares, each decorated with a letter of the alphabet. At naptime, each student chose a letter to sleep on. Mrs. Trinkner had a refrigerator full of ice cream and chocolate milk and she held me on her lap while she read aloud from *The Wizard of Oz*. In Mrs. Trinker's classroom, I was special.

In Mother's room, we worked quietly at our desks copying the letters of the alphabet from models tacked up over the blackboard. Sometimes, we could hear Mrs. Shaw playing "Fur Elise" in the small room at the back of the school where she gave piano lessons.

Mama's work still draws praise in the community, even though she employed methods now considered archaic. When two children "picked" at one another, she would draw a chalk ring on the hardwood floor and tell them, "Get inside it and fight until you've had enough. Just go ahead and fight." Once, she snatched the American flag from its place on her desk, broke its staff in half, and used the splintered stick to spank my friend Ray's behind. I didn't watch; I stared through the windows, straining for the sound of Mrs. Shaw's piano.

One day, a few years ago when Mama was out of town, her gardener called. He was terribly excited about something on the radio, something about Mama. I was frightened until I realized he'd been listening to Paul Harvey's "The Rest of the Story," on which one of Mama's former students, now a nationally known speaker, revealed the source of her ambition. She said she had resolved in first grade that, if she ever got out of Hortense Cauthen's class, where her mouth was often taped shut for speaking out of turn, she would "never stop talking." The yardman liked this.

My "Rest of the Story" is about a girl named Dottie Howse, teacher's pet in my first grade class. Dottie's family moved to Alachua after the 1948-1949 school year was already underway. She was brought into our classroom, introduced, assigned a desk, and we were informed that her father had helped develop the atomic bomb. Mama told the whole class Dottie was the smartest student she had.

Dawdling in her empty classroom while my mother attended a faculty meeting, I ransacked Dottie's desk. I found a fifty-cent piece and took it with me when I walked down the lane and across the washed-out dirt road to Grandmother Strickland's.

I began feeling guilty before I even arrived so, as soon as Grandmother turned her back, I went up the lane, through the schoolyard, found an unlocked door, and reentered the darkening building to return Dottie's money. But I didn't just put the coin back in her desk; I sat down in her chair, put my hand in, and felt all around inside the desk's cubbyhole. I held each of her stubby pencils in my hand, straightened her sheets of construction paper at right angles, and rubbed my palms over a fingerpainting she'd done that day. Finally, I slid the coin all the way to the rear.

I sat in Dottie's chair and thought about being Dottie Howse, having brothers like hers who were named Danny and David, and a mother with long, black hair. I visualized them around their piano, all together, harmonizing inside their red brick home. I thought of her daddy, Mr. Howse, whom I knew to be a genius.

chapter 7:

Main Street, Alachua (*Oxford, Mississippi, 1991*)

She was old man Charlie Stephens's mother and she came down
here way back in the pioneer days and they had to live at night in the
stockades. They'd work in the fields in the daytime but the Indians
would slip in at night, so they had to live in that stockade.

Said "One day a little Indian boy came up," and they took him in
and they kept him there for several years and fed him good and clothed
him. Said every evening, just before sundown, he'd climb up on the top
of the fence and give what they call the Indian 'warhoo.' You know, he'd
holler. And you could hear him a mile from there. That little Indian boy.
Lonesome for his people, you know.

When we was boys we would ask Old Lady Stephens—who got up
to nearly a hundred years old—ask her, say, "Miz Stephens, what about
the little Indian boy?" And she'd already told us a hundred times, but
little boys is children, you know. And she'd tell us again. Patient old
soul. And I'll never forget . . . Old Miz Stephens.

—Emery Williams, 1984[1]

When I left Florida in 1990 I was looking for emotional and intellectual
distance on Alachua, a perspective that might help me to comprehend the
abstractions behind the town's neat rows of houses and shops and its one stoplight.
I had sent the country chapters off to an agent, but withdrew them because I

realized they were meant to be part of a work that would not be finished until I wrote about the town. But I was too close, too involved, too married to the place; it felt as though Alachua—country and city—was as much me as my own flesh.

One night, while watching Bill Moyers interview religious historian Elaine Pagels on television, I decided to go back to school. I moved to Oxford in order to enter the graduate program in Southern studies at the University of Mississippi. This would, I thought, give me a fresh slate. I hadn't realized how foolish I'd feel sitting here and seeing, finally, that we're each issued only one. I thought I was beginning Chapter One of the second half of my life.

But after the long moving truck left Isom Place and I began to unpack, the life of Alachua rose up around me and spread through every room. Mere teacups held memories. I wanted distance on that Southern pocket I grew up in, but even three states away I can't look at a plate of barbecue or a Memphis Blues club except through the emotional lens I meant to leave behind—through that caul, Alachua, veiling my face. Despite all my wrestling against it, Alachua still weaves its relentless thread through each day, even in Mississippi.

Just blocks from the courthouse square Faulkner memorialized as "Jefferson," I've cleaned, painted, and even partially rewired a rented apartment in Isom Place, Oxford's oldest home. I've built in bookcases and against the wall, where during the Civil War Dr. Isom cached drugs so the Yankees couldn't find them, I've hung Mr. Chester Dampier's front porch door.

It's a keepsake, that door, a reminder of Mr. Dampier and all the other elderly men and women whose tape-recorded stories I've brought with me—Mary Lou, Vernon, Letha, all those who lived their lives within a sureness of flesh, field, and faith more reliable than my own. Most of those who entrusted me with their life accounts are already dead. Huldah Malphurs, who isn't, has sent me a letter: "It's a good thing you started working on that book while you were young," she says. "I don't believe you'd get done if you'd waited any longer."

Mr. Dampier's screen door came from his house in town that sat near the Church of Christ. The town's story could almost be told through its churches alone and not much would be missed, because its churches are Alachua's connective tissue. Before I left for Oxford, I tried many approaches, including the hire of a small plane in which the pilot and I zoomed low over the town's streets and churches at noon on a Sunday so I could examine the place from the air. I was close enough I could count the doll-like figures of Methodists descending the church's steps after their Sunday morning service, but I still didn't have the distance I needed. I decided it was too difficult; I couldn't explain the city. But, the truth is, until I write about the town, my own story is incomplete.

Over and over, I watch a movie of the earth's beginnings and, finally, staring into the antique LeMoyne /DeBry map of Florida, I realize that, although I can describe the peninsula's geography quite accurately, I must try again for perspective on Alachua, the town.

So, now, visualize Florida, its panhandle beneath Georgia and Alabama extending west, the peninsula swelling into a fullness of rivers and lakes. This is not the flat Florida reproduced in primary colors on a page in an atlas, but a land tumescent with underground streams that surface in springs given names as various as "Ginnie" and "Devil's Eye," springs from which millions of gallons of water bubble daily. This moist peninsula is lush with palmetto, oak, and palm, a world in which the scent of overripe mangos hangs in the languorous heat of summer and pink flowers rise like phalluses out of Queen Jasmine lilies in Alachua's front yards.

Millions of years before human migration started from the four river valleys of the Old World—the Tigris, Euphrates, Nile, and Ganges, according to my tenth grade world history teacher, Pat Robarts—a great trembling transformed our planet. Folds and ridges surfaced; separating, submerging, and uplifting, this enigmatic Earth thrust its molten interior into great mountain chains and valleys. Oceans appeared, and silvery-sliding rivers like our own Santa Fe yearned their way through the earth's epidermis. The limestone quarried west of town, our vine-thick hammocks, the nearby springs that rise and run into ribbony rivers, were all in place before the hunter-gatherer tribes arrived some 10,000 years ago.[2] What white men would name Latchua Country was untouched, complete, and self-sustaining before the Asian predecessors of Potano Woman

Detail of the LeMoyne/DeBry map of Florida. Sixteenth-century maps established land rights, spurring European exploration of the new world. Influenced by Indian guides and slave traders as well as by the impressions of French, Spanish, and British explorers, early mapmakers rendered the Florida peninsula in watercolors, paintings, pen and ink, woodcuts, and engravings, such as this remarkable rendering by Theodore DeBry from Jacques Morgues LeMoyne's original. The Frenchman, LeMoyne, who accompanied the Laudonniere Expedition of 1564, created *Floridae Americae Provinciae*, a map that speaks now to the mystery that Florida once was.[3]

are said to have crossed the Bering Strait and begun their centuries of journeying toward that day when one of them first examined the feathery fronds of *Zamia pumila*, the starchy Coontie plant.

It is difficult to imagine a time before we had so many unanswerable questions about nature and man's place withinin it. Most history texts suggest that history has primarily to do with humans, that man and nature are separate, a foolish notion for which the planet is currently offering correctives. We are not in right relationship, not with the earth or with one another.

Along a thousand miles of coastline, the surf murmurs like our mother's hearts heard in utero, its allure not merely glamorous as the travel ads would have it, but elemental. Drawn into Florida by the state's legendary beauty and mystery, five centuries of adventurers have pierced the peninsula's interior and, of course, radically modified it. I-75 tourists, on their way to the humming beaches, fly right past Alachua, 350 miles directly south of Atlanta, and I, for one, am grateful. Despite the stringent efforts of a few hometown boys turned developers, our voluptuous central highlands still provide homes for alligators and cottonmouth moccasins and sustain the fragile ecosystems they require. In this rich environment, mimosa trees spring up in untended corners of the town where the sweet scent of their pink blooms sings to us of locusts, honey, and Letha DeCoursey's African cousins.

For years, I have seen this city of 6,000 souls as unrelated to the landscape out of which it grew, its streets and buildings poor substitutes for the farmlands they replaced. Now I see that, when I viewed Alachua's grid and the countryside's wild harmony as opposites, I wasn't thinking deeply enough. After all, the town came into being as a trading center to serve surrounding rural communities such as Traxler. The town grew from the larger countryside, manifesting its ties in church dinners (now indoors and in air conditioning) and in numerous home gardens where cabbages, tomatoes, cucumbers, eggplants, beans, and squashes flourish.

Renovated Main Street storefronts obscure the riotous green and disorderly real life over which the city has been laid down, but that elemental past offers itself in random bits, even here. In sorting photographs, I have discovered a picture shot through a field of weeds that crowds up against the rear entrance of a commercial brick building. Crossing the building's back wall brick by brick, a fragment of the ancient hammock reasserts itself, tenacious, green. Extending its runners in a jagged line, a smilax vine moves inexorably up toward sky. Staring at this one green line, I realize that, however dissimilar, the town exists within—not separate from—the natural world. Reflecting on what is commonly regarded as a mere weed, one scrawling its way across the back of Mr. Sealey's dry goods store, weakens my view of country and town as opposites, as do my handwritten notes from a conversation with Mary Lou McFadden.

For a decade, I failed to recognize in my mother a potential informant. In turning away from Mother's concern for manners, I deafened myself to her voice—and to her—as a resource in understanding the town.

"Why don't you ask your mother about the mules at the ice plant?" Mary Lou asked one day, as I was quizzing her about them.

"My mother? You know my mother?"

Mary Lou knew Mother quite well; Mary Lou and her sister, Vernon, had driven a horse and buggy down the Bellamy Road in order to attend high school in town. They had tied up the buggy at my Strickland grandparents' house and Mother, a city girl, had been their classmate.

Fastened to my father by the fact of his death when I first returned in 1975, I haunted the dirt roads we had driven together, his father's farm in Monteocha, and our family graves at Antioch. Daddy's death divided past from present. Reliving what I had lost, I chose winding back roads over the town and its people. Seeking to hold on to my father, I preferred the countryside. But, now, in order to honor even the slenderest connections between country and city, I must give up my polarized view: male/female, country/city, black/white, old/young, us/them. I have to accept that it is not disloyal to my father to speak of the town or to attempt to love it, too.

The Cauthen Family gravestone at Antioch Cemetery, 1983.
Photograph by William A. Hunt. Used by permission.

I admit to the love-hate affair with place an Alachua minister once accused me of but, because I believe in the essential connectedness of all things, I am struggling to compose a narrative that will show me my true relatedness to the place I come from. Over my desk in Oxford, I have pinned a stanza from Auden's poem, "September 1, 1939," which reminds me of my susceptibility to negativity and despair and, most importantly, my resolve to write toward a destination in words that is, ultimately, affirmative.

From Mississippi, Alachua should appear a mere speck on the earth's face, its existence only a wink in the long, chronological corridor we call history, yet I spend whole days in Oxford peering into a blank computer screen searching for an understanding of the questions the town poses. I am yet Alachua's heretic daughter. Moving has not diminished Alachua's hold on me nor neutralized my ambivalence toward it.

The recorded voices of elderly people actually transport me there. Today, rain falls in sheets on three sides of the screened porch I added to the house where I lived for thirteen years. The rain slows, gray droplets swell at the edge of the roof and begin to fall in lines of clear beads, a curtain. Beyond the porch, a venerable dogwood still stands. In its lightning wounds, the woodpeckers tirelessly crochet intricate holes. Whole chunks of bark are missing, the branch that reaches toward the porch is leafless. In the side yard, the magnolia transplanted on my fortieth birthday flowers. Beneath the house-high wall of azaleas and fat, flowering trees, I buried compost for more than a decade. In the pink and white garden that will be punctuated with the red of Professor Sargent camellias next year, I have written poems, pulled weeds, drunk lemonade, made love, kept four pet chickens, and grown broccoli from seed. In August, hurricane lilies will bloom in a brief red streak where I planted them beneath the long hedge that reaches to the street. My desk looked out on that hedge. Without this hedge and the overgrown backyard, I could never have survived living in town. I was a farm girl and grew up with a horse to ride and whole fields to survey.

Alachua is, superficially, an undistinguished town. Older white families sustain genteel Southern habits that generally fail to impress newcomers; the black community is restive, but not yet assertive; I am told the air above the city is fouled by emissions from a boat factory; and citizens drink water no longer pristine. Like much of Florida, the town struggles to meet the demands of rocketing school populations and swelling numbers of workers buying into the new subdivisions. The University of Florida in Gainesville, the county's largest employer, is itself an agent of change. In interviewing elderly people, I learned of several who, in exchange for a life estate and a ten-dollar plaque, were persuaded to leave land to the University of Florida Foundation, a fundraising investment arm of the state educational system. How long, I wonder, will the beautiful hills above the Santa Fe River from which Earl Boston—descendant of one of Newnansville's first families—cut the trees for his own casket, be left unspoiled?

The town, Alachua, is younger than the rural hamlets marked by country stores and one-pump gas stops encircling it. Traxler, Bland, Santa Fe, LaCrosse, Monteocha, and Hague were named while Ft. Gilleland still stood at Newnansville. Alachua grew out of Newnansville, one of inland Florida's earliest communities. Because of the railroad's route, Newnansville exists now only as a cemetery, one and one-half miles east of town. Boston, Burnett, Colson, Dell, Mott, Olmstead, Pyles, Sanchez: the names on its oldest tombstones are those of homesteaders who lived here before Florida became a state, families who, during Indian uprisings, periodically fled their outlying farms for the protection of Newnansville.

Thriving and populous, Newnansville served as the county seat and, prior to the Civil War, was the location for a federal land grant office. During the Indian Wars of the 1800s, the outpost's population swelled to 1,500 persons while in Gainesville (later to become the county seat) the 1860s population was merely 223. Andrew Jackson was reputedly hated here, in part, says local historian Norm LaCoe, because Jackson said that the Florida women needed to " . . . . get rid of their cowardly husbands and marry men who would fight the Indians and tame the country."[4]

After the Savannah, Florida and Western Railroad laid rails to the southwest rather than at Newnansville, merchants and families took apart whole buildings and reassembled their wooden shops and homes near where the new railroad passed. They called the site "Alachua" and gradually replaced its wooden structures with brick ones. C. A. and Furman Williams, the father and uncle of Emery Williams who handed down "Old Miz Williams's" story of "the little Indian boy," filed Alachua's first plats, which laid out the streets and building lots of the new town.

Imagine today's curvilinear Main Street straight again, a flannelboard crowded with cutout images from a century of stories: dust clouds above marching elephants on circus day; Elijah Jenkins driving a mule pulling the city's one garbage wagon; Frazier Stephens carefully backing his long black Chalmers

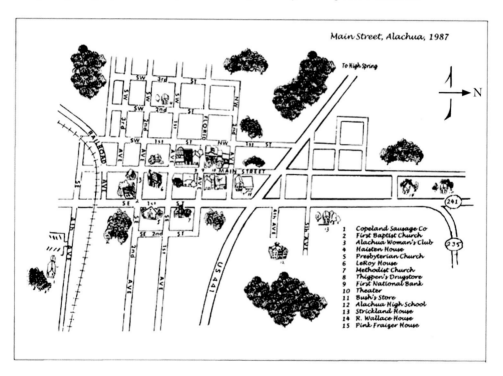

Main Street, Alachua, 1987. Map by Hal Cauthen (2006). Used by permission.

sedan into a tiny carriage house; small gas stations where gasoline is pumped into ten-gallon cylinders of clear glass, then allowed to drain back down into the cars; an Alachua described by one storekeeper as "a hub of civilization . . . one or two thousand people from several miles around [who] . . . did not see each other . . . except Saturdays, here in Alachua"; ten-year-old "Pink" Frazier carrying buckets of steaming milk downhill from DeWitt Hague's farm on a winter morning; one-armed taxi driver Bill Thomas, gesturing and steering his Model-A with the same hand; Lucile Ellis in a pickup truck filled with German shepherds; and brightly robed Hare Krishnas driving oxen in a Christmas parade. These disparate figures from different decades lay equal claim to the town. They all survive in a medium of accumulated stories, are nurtured in retellings, and endure.

My Strickland grandparents did not walk beneath Main Street's reproduction streetlights, but under hand-lit gas lamps. In imagination the past rewinds, flashing the Confederate victory at nearby Olustee, local fields once white with cotton, Grandmother Adeline Colson's forebears fighting in the Indian Wars, the Spanish, British, and French flags carried by men on foot, the muscular, tattooed physiques of Florida's aboriginal peoples and, even further, to the shaping of this earth they walked.

This, the locus of my imaginative life, appears to be just a simple, small, Southern town called by an old Indian name commonly said to mean "big jug without a bottom." Yet, even the town's name is given various pronunciations: La Chua, Elotchaway, Al-a-chu-ah. "Lotch-a-way," I hear most often, in the voices of the old women and men whose tapes I listen to in Mississippi.

Fulward Neeley told me that the bricks in Mr. Sealey's South Main Street building—placed side by side, end to end, curving in arches over the windows, were made of clay dug from pits at the south end of the county by Neeley's father, among others. When the bricks dried, they were removed from their forms, stacked, counted out in lots, and sold. They were loaded into wooden wagons and drawn by mules from the Campville Brick Company to this spot which was then little more than a field in farmlands previously cleared by an early settler.

These walls were built by anonymous workmen whose only signature is the work. Imagine one such man, muscled forearms gleaming in the hot sun of more than 100 years ago. His hands are scraped rough, for all day he lifts, places, and settles bricks into their mortar beds. Mortar clings in the hairs on the backs of his hands, sticks under his nails, and dries to a chalky gray. The vulnerable insides of his wrists are red with the day's scratches.

Front entrance to Mr. Sealey's mercantile (dry goods) store on South Main Street, Alachua, 1987. Photograph © Barbara G. Gibbs. Used by permission.

The mule-drawn wagons were unloaded, bricks placed in piles, and mortar mixed by men working from a book of plans that ensured that Alachua's Main Street design, like many Midwestern main streets being created at the same time, would repeat patterns in old buildings across the Atlantic. I like to imagine the grandson of our muscled workman returning from a world war to stroll about his hometown; he might have looked up at these windows called "Romanesque" and thought for a moment of light on the walls of Roman ruins.

Similar red bricks were used in the pillars, front porch facade, and chimneys of my Alachua bungalow built by George Duke in 1926. Its screened back porch was my favorite spot for reflection, but I also loved the interior of the house for the stories it told. In the shine of its floors, I saw the long, glistening needles of the trees Duke Lumber Company began harvesting in 1922 and, eventually, the loss of Alachua's virgin stands of yellow pine.

The first sawmill was not far from the house; its owner, George Duke, could hear the first of its four daily whistles from the kitchen table as he drank his morning coffee. Although South Main Street would not have been on Mr. Duke's route to the mill, it's only a few blocks away.

Mr. Sealey's store looked out on railroad tracks that curve out of sight in the direction of the old mill. Today, a modern train whistles past, carrying coal to the Deerhaven Electric Plant, jarring pictures off walls in the middle of the night, but not stopping. Trains once brought everything, including the mail. That was before automobiles, when the squat white building of today's Enneis Motor Company on South Main was still a cotton warehouse next to one of the town's three gins.

After the boll weevil destroyed their one-crop economy, farmers diversified: sweet and Irish potatoes, cucumbers, corn, and melons were hauled in from the countryside and packed at a shed built where the gin had stood. At the city-owned ice plant next door, the vegetables were iced down for transport and loaded onto trains.

The city's offices are no longer on Main Street; they have been relocated to the north, near US 441. The two-cell jail, the water tower rumored to be filled with snakes, and a cluster of boardinghouses are gone. The railroad—its route the impetus for the town's very beginnings—now does no business here.

Scattered along the south end of Main Street are the LeRoy house with its fish-scale shingles and leaded Gothic windows, the Dr. Bishop house, and three other Queen Anne homes with wide verandas. This architecture startles visitors who know nothing of the wealth produced by the area's early cotton plantations and who have not heard the stories of our old people. The LeRoy home has gas lights, Jenny Lind spool beds, Italian Carrara glass fireplace tiles of rose and green, and four-foot-wide moldings that are all one piece.

From Emery Williams's account of the early 1900s, I can visualize the tall, dark-suited Dr. James Bishop: his lanky figure leaves the house, walks to the curb, turns his head to the side, and spits. Tobacco spittle clears the width of the street, delighting a coterie of small boys who will make a legend of Bishop's skill. The McFadden sisters also have affectionate recollections of Dr. Bishop. They have shown me their little-girl likenesses caught in sepia, a picture taken in the Bishop cupola by a travelling photographer before whom Mary Lou and Vernon posed with their hair in sausage curls, wearing long dresses that reached to their toes.

At the beginning of the twentieth century, this now nearly deserted south end of Main Street rumbled with cotton gin and railway traffic and, by the 1930s, it was even busier, with trucks hauling trees to be sawed at Duke's mill and squealing pigs to be butchered at the Copeland Sausage Plant. The sawmill and meat packing companies were, for many years, the town's principal industries. Until recently, a concrete Rebel colonel stood at Copeland's gate.

That young boy carrying a fifteen-pound block of ice by the twine tied around it is Pink Frazier, on his way home. A meat market, selling beef heads and cow tails for fifteen cents apiece, is crowded. In the recessed doorways of the old brick commercial block, customers busily enter and depart. The fan-shaped Richardsonian windows are still lit. Not now, of course; not today. These details are from the stories. In 1991, this end of Main Street is empty.

Main Street was straight as a stick until a few years ago, but in its current incarnation its middle section has been made curvilinear and planted with young pear trees that will blossom in spring. It was not paved for automobiles until 1926, when federal money made it part of a system of roads called the Dixie Highway (which in 1936 became US 441). Regarding those workers employed for the road work, old-timer Chester Dampier, who read the *Wall Street Journal* every day of his adult life and took me down into the bomb shelter he built in the 1950s, said flatly, "It was a government job. If they could lean up on a shovel, they got paid." Earlier in the twentieth century, mules and horses pulling wagons and buggies were tied up under fat oaks that stood in a tall line along the dirt main street.

During the 1930s, customers selected live chickens from pens behind the small family stores in the center of town and carried them inside for weighing. Inside the high-fronted store of Simon Haisten, now painted a bright yellow, I can almost feel the rough fibers of the twine used to wrap bones for soup in butcher paper. (Mr. Haisten also wrapped cash in butcher paper and hid it in the freezer.) Without looking, I can reach out and pick up the jar of hard, red candies that stood on the shelf behind Haisten's counter.

Until the 1960s, Dr. Joe Thigpen's drugstore—Lydia Pinkham on its shelves, gift sets of "Evening in Paris" Perfume in blue bottles, and rhinestone jewelry in the glass display case—was a gathering place for teenagers who drank ten-cent Cokes at its black-and-white marble counters. Behind the drugstore, on Florida Avenue, were a barbershop, a blacksmith, and a stable. The blacksmith is no longer there and DeWitt Hague's mule stable burned. Of the three, only the shop where for sixty years my Uncle Willie cut hair is functional, a red-and-blue barber pole still turning beside the door.

Forty years ago the shelves that lined the barbershop's walls were filled with tall bottles of shaving lotion and blue tin cans of Jeris Talcum Powder. I often sat on an adult-sized bench, waiting for Daddy (who worked as a barber in order to support his real love, our farm) to finish his day's work and, if I pulled my feet up underneath me in a way he considered unladylike, Daddy communicated his disapproval over the head of the man he was shaving. Both long walls were mirrored, so that Uncle Willie, all the customers, and Daddy's grimaces reflected

90

in multiples. When Uncle Willie pumped the foot pedal to elevate his customers, his chair hissed over the voices of townspeople trading stories but, except for interruptions occasioned by ball game scores and weather reports, talk flowed unimpeded. For these two things only, storytelling stopped while all the men bent their heads towards the small, brown radio with two knobs that sat beside the cash register.

Many years ago a man with a policeman chasing him raced into the shop, ran past Uncle Willie and his waiting customers, and jerked aside the fabric that curtained only a toilet at the back of the room. Desperate, the man turned around and headed back through the shop's front (and only) door. When the policeman fired two shots, all the customers leapt up and dashed at the curtain, only to find, as the fleeing man had, that there was no opening in the wall behind. Uncle Willie was a great storyteller and, in his version, he never stopped clipping hair.

Uncle Willie loved three things: coon dogs, cigars, and work. Or perhaps it was money he loved. It was said that he got two dollars for every one he lent out to the blacks in town, and he was rumored to have had $10,000 in the bank before he was twenty years old. Although he was quick to provide funds for lighting the school baseball field and bought me a million Cokes, I once heard him declare he would not replace a home bathroom hot water faucet that had just that moment come off in his hand. "Shoot!" he said, "If I spend that money, I won't have it." He was known to carry a wallet full of bills.

One evening in 1974, my daddy, out on the short walk his doctor allowed him each day, came into the shop and found Uncle Willie, robbed and bloodied about the head, lying unconscious on the floor in front of his open cash register. The robber's weapon, a heavy iron pipe, was at his side. Uncle Willie nearly died that night and Daddy, already in his final illness, grew terribly disturbed, inserting "Willie, bloody as a beef" into every conversation until his death six months later. Eleven years after this robbery, Uncle Willie had seizures at the site of this same head injury and suffered brain damage that led directly to his death.

The town ignores its tallest building, an old theater shell. The theater's arched entrances were recently boarded up with plywood, and it has stood empty in the exact middle of Main Street for more than thirty years. Sitting here, my friends and I heard "Zippidy-doo-dah, Zippidy-ay, won-der-ful feeling, wonderful day" and "Off to see the wiz-ard," first met Hopalong Cassidy and the Lone Ranger, Brer Rabbit and Brer Fox. Here, I first held my breath as the lights went down and waited to see if the boy beside me would take my hand. Blacks sat in an upstairs balcony until the theater closed in the 1960s.

Contemplating this from Oxford, in 1991, it occurs to me that perhaps neither this theater nor any other will open until black and white Alachuans are ready to sit together. A 1982 poll of city residents revealed that, although a public swimming pool rated high on the civic wish list, no one wanted integrated swimming. Since then, other aspects of the city recreation program have flourished. Alachua's Pop Warner baseball team was named first in the nation, but there is still no pool.

In the theater's front wall are three arched windows, one closed with cement blocks. Vines cover its interior walls; rubble and weeds are the floor and the sky its ceiling. During my thirteen adult years in Alachua, sometimes in the evenings after dark I walked down and ducked in through a hole in the rear of the building. For me, the theater was still busy with images: the witch frightening Dorothy, the reliable face of Tonto, and the romantic image of Ginger Rogers and Fred Astaire. I would sit down, lean my head back against the wall, and, from inside the dark shell, watch the nighttime workings of the town.

On either side of the theater are shops with recessed doorways and a trim that looks like teeth where the buildings' top edges touch the sky. On the south is a shop where paunchy, dark-eyed Mr. Braswell waited behind a glass counter displaying ladies' hats and gloves. People told me he was a "Jew," an item of information I immediately matched to what the preacher's wife once emphasized at the Baptist Girls' Auxiliary Meeting. "Jesus was a Jew," she said, eyes glistening. Every time I passed the store I imagined Jesus on his cross in its dark interior.

On the north side of the theater, Mr. Rooks sat on a barrel, working the cash register and talking with customers in the little grocery that had belonged to his wife's father, Mr. Harris. Well before Harris came, my Uncle Colson worked here for W. T. Robarts who, when he needed more space after adding caskets to his hardware inventory, moved to the far south end of Main Street, where he added guns as well. Today, large red letters spell "KARATE" on the face of this building and behind its plate-glass window young boys in white split the air with their feet and fists. One afternoon more than forty years ago, Mr. Rooks detained me for what seemed like days while he tried to convince me not to leave Alachua after I finished high school. We were losing all our young people, he said. Finally, I told him what I thought: "This place doesn't interest me in the least."

Middle Main Street is a panoply of horrors for a historic preservation purist: double antique doors replaced by a modern one of glass with concrete block filled in on either side; beaded ceilings obscured by lower ones of asbestos tiles to save on heating costs; and air conditioners blocking front door transoms designed for air circulation—these abound. The largest, most flourishing business on the street is "Conestogas" [sic], a restaurant featuring steak, burgers, and "buffalo wings." Its decor is Western, with saddles, harnesses, and hats. On the walls in photographs, covered wagons cross deserts and cowboys herd bison against Western mountain ranges. There is a wonderful irony in these pictures because Florida's pioneer cowmen, though not the subject of movies, did the same work.

In 1989, the last year I lived in Alachua, the Chamber of Commerce named as "Businessman of the Year" and presented a plaque "for efforts to preserve Alachua's heritage" to the very man who, in my view, defiled the street's history. This individual renovated many buildings, then erected a celebratory sign near US 441, directing people downtown. "Historic Downtown Alachua" his sign reads, heralding the perhaps unintentional destruction of much of what once actually was historic.

Nothing more clearly proclaims how racially divided Alachua is than the separation of Main Street's north end from its middle and south ends. The three sections are altogether no more than a mile in length, but the northern third, called "North Main," which is all black and residential, lies on the other side of Highway 441's four lanes. For the casual visitor and the casual white resident alike, the east end doesn't exist. The visitor often mistakes active US 441 for the entirety of Main Street and, if merely driving through, does not notice the identifying, white concrete post on the corner lettered "MLK Blvd" for Martin Luther King, Jr. Indeed, until 1984 I had, myself, failed to recognize that Main Street extended beyond US 441.[5]

Here stand no commercial brick buildings with trim set like teeth against the sky, no fish-scale shingles, leaded windows, or wide porches. The porch I sit on here is barely the width of a chair. This street has no Romanesque, Queen Anne, or Italianate details, nothing commercial unless (and this is not unlikely) a crack cocaine dealer has set up in one of these small, unpainted houses. Here, beyond US 441, Main Street consists of simple dwellings, small vegetable gardens, and children at play. It appears mundane, yet pulses with stories.

The city first paved the north section of Main Street in 1990. Since the early 1900s, it had been a bumpy road of potholes and sleeping dogs, a dusty path fading into a thicket where the bitter-smelling flowers of orange lantana and lion's ear bloomed. At the back of "Pink" Frazier's property in a pig pen sat the old red pick-up Uncle Willie got too sick to drive. Probably some of the swine had been his, too.

After selling barbeque and soliciting donations up and down this and adjoining streets for many years, black visionary Jack Postell realized a long-held dream when the Alachua County Training School was finally established for the education of black children in 1922. When Joe Louis won the world heavyweight boxing title in 1937, a white man living on this street cursed and threw his radio out through the living room window. Towards High Springs, in what was once woods, then pasture, the sun sets behind the new Food Lion Shopping Center.

Around the corner is St. Matthew's, which grew out of Old Shiloh, a church created during Reconstruction when blacks left biracial churches and established their own. Here, I joined the congregation and its pastor in a creative call and response and, for a documentary videotape, Deacon Charles Lawson beamed me one of the dearest smiles I've ever seen. Asked about Alachua's future, he replied, "It has not yet appeared what we shall become."

94

Near St. Matthew's sits the home of Letha DeCoursey's sister, Rebecca Wallace, who grew up to become a midwife. For the births of more than 1,500 babies over fifty-nine years, Rebecca snatched up coat, satchel, and chalk each time she left for work and scratched out on a front porch chalkboard the address to which she was going. Rebecca always left her door unlocked. Often, when she returned, she found payments in the form of hogs' heads or buckets of peas on her kitchen table.

It must always have been there, but I never truly saw the north end of Main Street until the day I first went up it on my way to interview eighty-seven-year-old Rebecca. She invited me into her living room and brought out a box. Along the length of her couch, we spread several generations of baby photos, school pictures and formal portraits, snapshots of houses, cars, and graves. She even had a picture of the man who arrived each spring in a wagon drawn by goats along the shoulder of the road. When I asked if she had any photos of herself, Rebecca took both my hands in hers and looked into my eyes, as though trying to discern my character. Then she told me to wait, stood up, and went into a side room.

From where I was sitting, I watched her step nimbly up onto her pink bedspread. From above the head of the bed she took down an oval frame and, holding it against her chest, climbed carefully down. Without a word, she came back into the room and pressed into my hands a large, tinted photo of herself and her two sisters in long dresses, three young women smiling at a photographer from the edge of a cotton field. The nosegays they held, she remembered, had been picked from the side of the road after the photographer appeared. "You can take it," she said, thrusting the formal photograph at me. "And those," she nodded, indicating all the other pictures spread out on the couch.

White women I had known all my life would not lend photographs so I could copy them, but this frail black woman with enormous eyes trusted me. I thought for a minute: my mother had grown up in a house one street over. Mother was six years younger than this woman, but more significant than the difference in age was their difference in color. I supposed they had not played together as children.

"Did you ever know my grandparents, the Stricklands?" I asked doubtfully.

Her black eyes regarded me thoughtfully. "Who your mother?"

"Hortense", I answered. "Hortense is my mother."

"I used to help your grandmother," Rebecca replied. "I named my first grandbaby 'Hortense' for your mother."

Back in my Alachua house, I centered the framed picture of the three young women above my bed. I thought of black Mattie Richardson who had cared for me and called me "Dollbaby" when I was a preschooler, and her daughter, Carrie, who was one of my first playmates. I thought, too, of Jacqui Moorer, who had sat with me at "the stump" where whites said only the most notorious black folk gathered. Jacqui had braved the black tent revival with me; her father, Alex Lundy, bathed my father in his last illness; and, when my Aunt Tomye died, I called Jacqui first.

Rebecca's telling me of the naming of her granddaughter had joined us as surely as a straight line drawn between the connecting dots of her house and my grandmother's, one street over. We were fastened together, kin. In one sentence, this small woman with piercing eyes had enlarged my world: blacks, as well as whites, now peopled the city. The unconscious racism that had blinded me was gone and I saw that Mattie and Carrie and Jacqui and Alex were not peripheral, but integral, to my world.

From Oxford, Mississippi, I cannot see the clouds that hung above Rebecca's street that day in 1984 or the cracks between the boards of her wooden floors. Distance has obscured these details but thrown into relief the gift I was given. As long as blacks were invisible, there was a part of myself to which I didn't have access; a stolen part of me had been handed back.

c h a p t e r   8:

A Good Little Piece to Go (*Oxford, Mississippi, 1992*)

> My vision requires among us in Alachua a spiritual renewal, and
> to speak of renewal is to speak of the quality of relationships . . .
> we need to have the love that Mr. Lawson spoke of, that crosses and
> even erases racial lines. I will say this: I have been to a black church
> here in Alachua and I was treated like a queen, absolutely like a queen.
> And that puts a lot of people to shame [who] are the same color I am.
> —Marilyn Escue, 1983[1]

The quality of relationships between blacks and whites revealed itself as
at the heart of Alachua's concerns over the course of nine town meetings in
which heritage, work, education, family values, newcomers, health, recreation,
government, and religion were discussed. Blacks were vocal; several remarked
that this was their first opportunity to make themselves heard in the larger
community and that they were grateful for it. In 1983, when African-Americans
comprised fifty-one percent of the city's population, Alachuans painted a self-
portrait in words, clearly telling us that unresolved issues of race clouded all
aspects of the town's churches, schools, and politics. We were divided by race.

The Churches

As soon as I got near his rocking chair with my tape recorder, storyteller
Emery Williams said, "You can't talk about Alachua without talking about

Newnansville." It's also true we can't grasp present-day Alachua without talking about its churches, beginning with Florida's first Methodist church, established at Newnansville in 1822. Indeed, because it has nearly two dozen, some call Alachua "a city of churches."

A 1930s document, "The Fifth Revision of a Historical Sketch of Methodism in Alachua" by W. T. Robarts, has come into my possession. This startling piece speaks of "The Southerner, who had brought them the first step of the way from [the] savagery and cannibalism of the African jungles . . . ." "Them" refers to Alachua's newly emancipated blacks, whose description in these faded pages not only testifies to longstanding racial biases, but also provides a record of white settlers' attitudes toward former slaves many years after the end of the Civil War. Against this history, we can measure just how far we have come in our ongoing struggles with race. And, as Robarts says in his essay, "The town began with its churches."

There is no way to ascertain what parts of the Methodist "sketch" the lanky undertaker W. T. Robarts inherited or which section best reflects his own views but, without a doubt, the revision employs language any contemporary schoolchild would recognize as backward; its dated tone dramatizes how greatly the way we talk about race has changed since the 1930s. In our struggles with race, perhaps the "sketch" gives us something to measure against.

First, reports Robarts, the settlers built a house of worship, as that "is the American way and . . . since the landing of the Pilgrim fathers . . . the church invariably became the community center." That's obvious, really, and of course opinions were formed as church members squinted through ministerial interpretations of the *Bible*, especially during the Civil War when preachers regularly cited scripture to justify slavery. Robarts's church history speaks of the "tragedy, adventure, romance of the knightly pioneers" who were "stalwart, heroic, good," and "assembled in groups . . . like knights of old." Though blacks and whites worshipped together in antebellum Newnansville, during Reconstruction blacks established their own churches, such as St. Matthew's Baptist, the church attended by Letha DeCoursey and her sister, Rebecca Wallace.

The isolation of pioneer settlements and the concomitant lack of social and intellectual stimulation account for the central role Southern evangelical Protestantism played in the region's thought, how even today a nearly homogeneous worldview finds expression in Alachua's classrooms and voting booths. Churches have always been influential in the American South and in the early 1800s, when men, women, and children lived on farms miles apart without phones or radios, it could not have been otherwise.[2] Although I very much doubt a woman would have compared herself to a "knight of old," by the end of the nineteenth century my widowed great-grandmother Adelaide Mott Colson (Holder), who battled laundry with a stout stick and made her own lye soap on a farm near the Santa Fe River, probably took her political cues from church leaders. And she surely looked forward to Sunday not only as a day of duty, but as a break from the week's relentless physical labor, a chance to socialize over pots of chicken pileau (pronounced "pur-low") and the wild venison roasts that, after the morning sermon, were set out along a makeshift table on New Hope Baptist's shaded church lawn.

A casual (white) reader might at first consider Robarts and/or the revisionists before him merely sentimental—until she reads that "the [Civil] War was not so difficult as afterward when slaves had the vote and the populace was subjected to 'ignorance, superstition, and savagery' and the situation required 'more than a decade before the lines of color could be drawn and protection to society restored in order to meet the ideals of the true southerner.'" The tone of this description demonstrates how, during Reconstruction, white Southerners adopted racist views that became the accepted wisdom of a people who feared losing the Civil War would mean the dismantling of their entire culture—a culture built on the labor of slaves in a plantation economy.[3]

Reading his first lines, I felt a measure of sympathy for Robarts's sense of loss and sadness, his insistence that traditions be preserved, but my true Southerner's eyes bulged right out over my cheeks as I read that "the newly franchised negro citizenship [needed the guidance of] their best friends, the Southerner, who had brought them the first step from the savagery and cannibalism of the African jungles." That's not the way it was, of course, and today this language astounds. At least there is that.

In 1981, after an absence of nearly twenty years, I returned to Alachua's First Baptist Church for a Sunday morning service. I knew that church leaders, particularly Methodist and Baptist, exert a huge influence on the policies of the town. They sometimes pressure church members about non-religious issues. I was a high schooler when deacons threatened a recalcitrant church officer with the loss of his local government job. I was bewildered, because Azilee Cumbee and Pat Robarts who taught history had pounded into my head that church and state are separate. Now I know the mindset of evangelicals throughout the South encourages no such distinction. Further, unlike belief systems which interpret duty to God as including, also, duty to one's earthly brothers and sisters, Southern evangelical Protestantism understands duty chiefly as the responsibility for saving individual souls. So focused on salvation is this tradition that it is theoretically possible to save a beggar's soul and walk away jubilant, leaving a "saved" person hungry in the street. This worldview encourages the complacency of "Once saved, always saved" that renders a social Gospel superfluous, after which one can do just about anything (or nothing) with impunity.

The same evening Marilyn Escue described how she was welcomed into black churches, black educator Leoris Richardson took issue with policies of segregation at white churches. "I was sitting here," Leoris said, bending toward her audience with a radiant smile,

> listening to all the beautiful remarks and was thinking, Just what will happen tomorrow? Tonight we are united. What will happen if blacks come into the [white] First Methodist Church and join there? And tonight, what a beautiful sound it was to have all of you sing 'Amazing Grace.' No one knew what color we were if they were outside the door.

While local Hare Krishnas served vegetarian refreshments following the meeting, Richardson was mobbed by enthusiastic white youngsters.

It was true; we had indeed sung "Amazing Grace" together. Even more surprising was our conspicuous enjoyment of music and refreshments furnished by the Krishnas, heretofore acknowledged only in the annual Christmas Parade. As heads bobbed and voices blithely sang along to the beat of drums and clashing cymbals, I grew embarrassed that, after receiving two telephone threats against the Krishnas, I'd notified the police to stand by. Then I remembered that in Alachua manners are everything.

Despite my fears of public dissension, that night's discussion of religion addressed longstanding discrepancies between Alachuans' stated beliefs and their behaviors; theirs is a Sunday religion seemingly absent from weekday practice. Speakers spoke pointedly of a need for interracial understanding in an Alachua that, in its beginnings, was stereotypically Southern—set in its ways, defensive, and unwilling to be self-critical. Fifty years after Robarts delivered his revised sketch at a Methodist homecoming, Jim Kelly made this observation:

> The more different kinds of people that you actually can like and love, you're better off for it. If you don't like, if you can't stand blacks, or if you can't stand Yankees, or you can't stand rednecks, or you can't stand . . . you know, some religious thing or whatever . . . you're the one that's suffering. You're the one that's hurting. Not them.

The Schools

The night we discussed education in the town hall, several black schoolteachers spoke up. St. Elmo Cherry told how, growing up in a racially divided Alachua, she was trained by her parents to challenge the cultural assumptions that, otherwise, would limit her success:

I remember a certain kind of attitude would prevail that, if you were born black in America, you could only achieve so much. My daddy's attitude was that that may be true, but you go as far as you can within the system. His attitude was there are ways to get what you want, but you have got to know how to play the game. And I remember him saying that everything is survival. When you learn how to survive in an integrated society or a segregated society, let those experiences teach. Let your negative experiences—racism or whatever you want to call it . . . [teach]. So I had the kind of orientation to forge ahead in spite of the odds.

Not only had I grown up blissfully unaware of the racism that shaped both our lives, I'd never before heard Cherry's family name.

Black Mary Jones stated that, since integration, discipline had become a larger problem in schools. Cherry agreed. Then a third black teacher, soft-spoken Thelma Welch, spoke up:

> When they integrated at Mebane, I was teaching there and I had the music program and I was very disillusioned. And I guess that, when you have something on your chest, you want to get it off; I think this is the time to get it off. I had been teaching music there and, when they integrated, the high school went to Santa Fe. There were some brand new choir robes which had been purchased the year before integration, and I was going to use these robes with the chorus at Mebane . . . And when I gave each of these robes out, their parents sent me a note that the children could not wear them, and that hurts me. They had been worn by the black chorus children, and I had a lot of whites in the choir. Those robes rotted because I could not use them. And I wonder if the parents would have thought about what they were doing when they told these kids they could not wear them because they had been worn by black high school children. I would have had them cleaned.

Even now, reading this hurts. Thelma Welch had given me piano lessons; she'd introduced me to a song that begins, "Let there be peace on earth and let it begin with me." Perhaps equally significant, she had shared her piano stool; on it we sat together, threw back our heads, and sang, "And then they nursed it, rehearsed it/and gave out the news/that the Southland/gave birth to the Blues."

A professor of nursing whose students interned at elementary schools in Alachua and nearby High Springs compared racial attitudes; she told us that, in High Springs, black and white children play together and eat happily at the same table. In contrast, "When you go to Mebane you can feel the racial hostility."[4]

Listening from the audience, I considered the implications: did some stigma still attach to Mebane because, even though now integrated, it was first used, like the choir robes, by blacks? I knew from conversations with local teachers that an assignment to Mebane was often seen as a punishment. In the city hall meeting room, most listeners' faces were bland. A few glanced behind their chairs as though looking for something, then turned back around and crossed their arms over their chests.

Cherry was direct, even vehement, then she stopped; as though intuiting discomfort in her audience, she offered a deeper level of explanation, a confidence:

> I am going to tell you something else that integration has taught me:
> it taught me how to play the game. I learned I could not be my
> black self. Because people could not understand my behavior, I was
> misinterpreted. My intensity was viewed as anger, hostility, and
> aggression—such emotions as caring and concern and feeling strong
> and speaking out. So integration taught me cultural differences that
> I was not even aware of because I had stayed on one side of town
> so long.

Only three white people walked out while Cherry was speaking, but dozens (including my own mother) called the next day to tell me they would not attend subsequent meetings if Cherry were scheduled to speak. Blacks called to say they supported Cherry; she told the truth.

The anger and hurt expressed by blacks at this session were not so surprising to me as the discomfort whites demonstrated in reaction to Cherry's comments. She had indicated her point of view at our initial meeting when she alluded to "growing up on one side of town." Years later, what I saw as Cherry's honest intensity was quoted out of context during her campaign for a city commission seat she did not win.

The Politics

It's no wonder Cherry's election campaign, one of the first black attempts at election to the city commission, failed. Our politicians traditionally come out of white churches, almost always from Protestant denominations, and many are accomplished church leaders before they announce themselves as candidates for public office. An amazing presentation by Ralph Cellon, Jr., himself a Baptist deacon, former city commissioner, and celebrated public speaker, made this obvious.

Cellon appeared as an inducement aimed at potential audiences. In his "roast" of historical figures in Alachua's city government, he described the overlapping intricacies of politics, business, and church leadership before a mixed audience sitting in rows of uncomfortable chairs at city hall. Our town's leaders, Cellon said, are "sort of a benevolent group who were the city commission or fathers of the community . . . who mostly told us what was good for us." In the audience, someone grunted. Cellon continued:

> Preacher Copeland was the Grand Potentate or whatever. He signed the checks up there at the Copeland Sausage Company for a long time; and he got up in the pulpit and led them and did the preaching; and he told them everything they needed to know; and he was a jolly good guy.

Mel Phillips was another one: some of you probably never heard of that rascal. But Mel Phillips was in the Oliver Dealership down here. Well, anybody who would sell an Oliver Tractor, they cannot be trusted, anyway. He did not last very long, according to our records. He wanted to be on there [the city commission] to create a little business for himself, and he got to be a Baptist deacon for the same reason.

In front of me, a heavy man shifted his weight and his chair creaked. Others laughed uneasily, underscoring the possibility that Cellon's remarks (even though framed as humor) had struck home. The spectacle of a political figure and church official publicly presenting as a joke the unspoken and deepest suspicions of his audience was surely unexpected; they were rapt.

Cellon beamed and offered further details, characterizing the attitude of the man he called the "Grand Potentate," a Church of Christ minister who, in addition to his ministerial duties, also founded Copeland Sausage, one of the town's first sources of tax revenue:

> The way you keep somebody on the commission from Copeland Sausage Company is tell [the Copeland workers], "Hey! You-all want to work, stuff them chitlins and make them sausages, and all that? Well, this is who you vote for."

Cellon's talk was offered in a spirit of play, or I think it was. Nevertheless, his words underscore the historic reality of Alachua politics. It would be untrue to say all past commissioners in the City of Alachua thought or behaved identically, but for the better part of the twentieth century the decisions of the majority have kept political control in the hands of a few white men.

The character of all past commissioners' attitudes and behaviors finds expression in a composite fictional character I've invented.[5] I call him Foevrin Power, for the ideology he embodies has controlled the city since its incorporation in 1905. Foevrin has an aunt who is a secretary at City Hall. Her husband is a policeman and their son is city manager. Foevrin's brother-in-law's brother sits on the zoning board. Within these elaborate kinship connections, Foevrin finds governing easy, almost natural. And others concerned with city business, as it turns out, inevitably go hunting or play golf at the same times and in the same places Foevrin does. If he misses one of his buddies, he can find him, dressed in jeans and a cowboy hat, ruminating over cups of coffee at the Rebel Restaurant where Foevrin goes every weekday morning. Foevrin sees many of these people again, of course, as he fulfills his duties as a deacon at the First Baptist Church.

Immediately before city elections in the spring, Foevrin—still trim, wearing a polyester leisure suit and the enduring self-confidence of a man who was once a handsome high school football hero—can be seen driving his car up North Main Street, into an area he calls "the quarters." Here he is hailed with "Hi, Boss!" as he dispenses half-pint bottles of Captain Morgan Rum. In the years when his seat is contested (which does not happen often), it is said he also gives out one-dollar bills. He is adored by old ladies and children of both races.

Foevrin's ideology is simple belief in the American Dream and its tenets: hard work, morality, thrift, and, most importantly, that word he learned from the Yankees: "progress." Ironically, while maintaining a rebellious Southern pose, Foevrin has adopted a concept that derives directly from the Enlightenment and fueled the Industrial Revolution, one that has replaced the very independence and self-sufficiency his grandfather supposedly defended in the Civil War. Our prototype and his friends in the Chamber of Commerce have an abiding faith in "progress" (and probably understand the term to mean secular materialism rather than intellectual or moral improvement). Any proposal labeled "progress" gets a majority vote from the Chamber, the Lion's Club, and from the members of Foevrin's church; the zoning board's vote is unanimous.

One election morning a few years back, as I steered Uncle Willie towards a voting booth, Foevrin intercepted Uncle Willie's unsteady walk by stepping between us and the curtained space Uncle Willie was about to enter. According to law, candidates are not allowed in the polling place, but Foevrin, standing close enough to press the lever himself, stuck out his hand to Uncle Willie and said, "You know which stick to pull, don't you, Mr. Willie? Not going to forget your old buddy, Foevrin. Foevrin Power: first stick at the top!" In one of his last public moments, Uncle Willie entered the booth and then, all the way home, like the yeoman farmer he truly was, regaled me with a list of Foevrin's virtues: Foevrin, the "big man" who had stopped to speak.

Foevrin presided as mayor, one evening as courteously as an Edwardian gentleman, the next, gaveling down the crowd with the raw vulgarity of an Erskine Caldwell character. He was affable the night a state road department spokesman announced plans to cut down many of the old live oaks planted and watered by hand fifty years earlier by Huldah Malphurs's senior class. The cutting precipitated a furor: several individuals (including Aunt Tomye) threatened to block bulldozers with their bodies and, afterwards, a Sierra Club botanist inspected the cut trees and declared only a few had warranted removal because of disease. Yet, at City Hall Foevrin murmured to the road department man, "Thank you for coming to give us the good news."

For all this, it is devilishly difficult not to like Foevrin: the man pats babies, opens the post office door for old ladies, roots for the Florida Gators, and is the first person to visit when you land in the hospital. Finally, his speech has the indelible cadence and timbre of your own father and grandfather's, and love of that is not easily surrendered.

Does Foevrin realize his old world of privilege and order no longer exists? Have he and his culture learned anything from the South's legendary lessons of defeat? Or is Foevrin still convinced of his own superiority and in agreement with his wife who intercepted my 1987 door-to-door delivery of political campaign literature and in outrage declared, "You are a traitor to your own people!"

"Who do you mean 'my people'?" I asked. "The old, white families in Alachua?"

"Yes, that's who I mean."

"Have you looked at the voter registration roll lately?"

"I've seen it."

"Then you know that, out of 6,000 people, there are only about 300 voters left who represent old, white families. How long do you think 300 people can dictate to the rest of that 6,000?"

"Right on, I hope," she said, "and I'm ashamed of you."

Mama was out of town that day, but I could hear her speaking as clearly as though she stood right there: "You're going to get yourself talked about," she said.[6]

At the post office I once overheard a man exclaiming with disgust over the amount of his city utility bill. "Well, well," he said, "they just do whatever they feel like, don't they?" A moment later, face-to-face with "they," he blandly exchanged smiles and "howdy-dos" with a city commissioner. When I complained about city politics, Mother would say, "Try to think of something nice."

The cunning Foevrins who make deals and wield power may actually be more realistic than I about human nature, for they have neither had to study history nor go three states away to grasp at perspective; they look about them and watch one another. In my unwillingness to accept human rapacity as the norm, in wanting to remain innocent of that terrible knowledge, I, too, practice denial. But Foevrin is my brother, my sister, my mother, and my father—me, for I also admire neat stacks of monogrammed, starched linen; I want the leisure to read and think and, most of all—that greatest luxury—to reflect. I turn away from the realities of the commercial world and would like to avoid practical matters. So Foevrin, living in his memories, dreaming of the old privileged life, stands also for me.

Just Wherever You Were

We have come a distance from that Methodist history of the 1930s and from the climate in which my mother, on her tenth birthday, was given a plastic alligator whose open mouth held a pencil with a Negro head on the end of it. Toward the end of the series of town meetings, Mary Elizabeth Knight Irby and her son Will furnished us a contrast in perspectives. Here is a portion of Mrs. Irby's beautifully written account describing how visits to Alachua provided meaning for her mobile family when her father worked for the railroad during the 1920s and 1930s:

> We came by car and what I remember most about coming by car was a new road through a tall pine forest. It was like going down a hall. I can remember as a child looking down these long halls of pine trees and newcut roads. We came by train sometimes and sometimes we stayed with relatives. Sometimes we stayed at the Skirvin Boarding House . . . down near the railroad tracks, down near Enneis Ford place.
>
> We came to visit our family and to visit old friends that my parents cherished more than any others they had met anywhere. We came to help with cane grinding and hog killing. We came to the family reunions . . . to weddings and funerals and summer picnics at Burnett's Lake, when it was time to pick tobacco, harvest melons, pick corn, and go to the market.
>
> No matter where we lived, it was always thought of as a temporary residence, because someday we would be going back home. So my father's standard answer to "Where do you folks live?" was "Well, we are staying here right now, but our home is in Alachua."
>
> When we were in Alachua, "home" was just wherever you were. It was out at the farm. It was at the church. It was sipping lemonade and eating grape hull pie on my Aunt Clara Stephens's front porch. It was down at Willie's Barbershop, Braswell's Dry Goods Store, Haisten's Meat Market, Joiner's Drug Store, or at the post office. It did not matter.

Mrs. Irby's Alachua was a white one, but a similarly appreciative account might as easily have come from a black citizen who loves the place because it was loved first by his father and grandfather. It belongs to him, too, in a final and irrevocable sense that has nothing to do with deeds or titles to land.

Will Irby's remarks contrast with those of his mother; his reflect a consciousness formed by the challenging events that confronted him during the 1960s, when he delivered morning newspapers in Alachua.

I am looking at these newspaper headlines and I see that the President of the United States has been assassinated. People are marching on the capital. There are sit-ins. I see that the president's brother, Robert Kennedy, has been assassinated. I am delivering these papers and [nevertheless] the sun is coming up as usual over the City of Alachua, and I am starting to wonder why.

The headlines would tell us that Martin Luther King, Jr. had been assassinated [and] to go there each morning and look at the headline and go through this small town with the sun coming up as usual, to see all that was going on in the world and to see that many of the families that I would be delivering the papers to would be in a different home perhaps, next year, and it would be a better home than it was the year before, and the car might be a newer model. Things seemed to be going along pretty well here.

These statements from a mother and her son illustrate how greatly perception can shift in just one generation. Since 1983 when Will Irby described the Alachua of his boyhood in the 1960s, the elementary school population increased by fifty percent, from 632 to 916 in 1992. Newcomers still find surface Alachua safe and insular, especially when they drive our country roads winding through dense hammocks and rolling green pastures commonly dotted with red-and-white Hereford cattle. Although we now have two elementary schools, the quiet town surrounded by lush countryside encourages the illusion that escape from a too-fast world is possible. Northern transplants relax in the sunshine while old-timers stand fixed, visualizing past tea parties and counting their good, starched linen napkins into neat stacks. Escape is only a dream, of course. Late twentieth-century violence and pessimism are not confined to what arrives via television; they are expressed also in rumors of raw sewage leaks, a thriving drug trade, and a poverty both physical and spiritual.

Marilyn Escue's statement of vision mentioned "the love that Mr. Lawson spoke of." Immediately before Escue's remarks, Deacon Charles Lawson of St. Matthew's Baptist Church spoke directly to my own concern, the habitual divorcing of religious belief from secular behavior:

> I would like to take out one word here and work off it, and that word is `religion.' You deal with people who want to think that religion is something that you get. But, really, it is something that you keep. You must keep it. You have got to keep it.
>
> This genuine religion is based on love . . . . This love, it is something that moves about . . . and, when we keep this religion, we live it in our homes, we live it in the community. We live it in our churches, we teach it everywhere we go. We have got a good little piece to go yet, because it has not yet appeared what we should be like.

Years later, paging to 1 John 3:2 in Granddaddy Strickland's worn *Bible* (page 1313), I thought of the gentle Lawson as I read:

> Beloved, now are we the sons of God, and it doth not yet appear what we shall be: but we know that, when he shall appear, we shall be like him; for we shall see him as he is.

There is "a good little piece to go yet." And we have heard their voices:

> I have been to a black church . . . and I was treated like a queen . . . . The more different people that you can actually like and love . . . . The children could not wear them [and] those robes rotted . . . . Integration has taught me [that] I could not be my black self . . . . You-all want to

work, stuff them chitlins and make them sausages, and all that . . . .
traitor to your own people . . . . home was just wherever you were . . .
It was at the church . . . sipping lemonade and eating grape hull pie on
my Aunt Clara Stephens's front porch. . . . The sun is coming up as
usual over the City of Alachua, and I am starting to wonder why . . . .
Genuine religion is based on love . . . something that moves about . . .
and when we keep this religion . . . we teach it everywhere we go.

Decoding the past, I hold in my hand the 1959 Santa Fe High School
prom program showing a hoop-skirted girl on the deck of a river boat. I asked
my classmate Johnny Thomas for that design, unconsciously putting forward an
emblem of plantation culture. And that same year I was mystified when my friend
Annie spoke passionately in class about the unfairness of segregation. I thought
she held a peculiar view.

Shortly after the 1954 Supreme Court decision, *Brown v. Board of
Education*, our county school board postponed integration in Alachua by first
creating Mebane High School for blacks. In September 1956, I was at a brand-
new school for whites, Santa Fe High, the scratch of wool trousers against my
thighs as I and seventy-five other band members marched onto the football
field for a Friday night pre-game show. Our lines were straight, our drummers's
sticks hitting snare drum rims in unison, and up front leading us was seven-foot-
tall Jimmy Kinnard wearing another two feet of strapped-on drum major's hat.
Kinnard, three dozen majorettes, and the first ten rows of our historic red and
gray uniforms crossed the forty-yard line before Jimmy's lips closed on the blood-
curdling yell we were known for. We were, after all, the Rebels.

As I am writing, I see out my window the Mississippi lawn turning a pale
green in the late afternoon light. Hundreds of miles to the southeast, the Bellamy
Road is "dusk-dark," the crickets have quit, and the falling orange ball we call a
"sun" disappeared an hour ago behind Mary Lou and Vernon's old barn. The same
night encloses Alachua and Oxford; both share the same permeable sky.

In Alachua, a white line of street lights curves from US 441, south, towards what was once Mr. Sealey's dry goods store and the Women's Club built beside it on South Main.[7] I first read the club prayer a few years ago when Mother's friend asked me to proofread a revision of the club's by-laws. After I corrected all the grammatical stuff, I lightly penciled in a question mark at the end of the line describing potential members as "white women of good character."

At the clubhouse tonight, women of all ages are parking their cars, getting out, and climbing up the steps. The women have worked all day in offices, teaching school, working in hospitals, or caring for children and old people at home. They fed their families supper only an hour ago. Some have driven into Alachua's quiet streets by way of the Bland, LaCrosse, and Hague roads, along which the black-eyed Susans, prickly lavender thistles, and pale-faced primroses bloom. The women arrive, repeating a pattern their mothers and grandmothers established in earlier gatherings in this spacious structure built by WPA labor with stone from nearby fields.

A hand-stitched cloth of lace and linen squares covers the refreshment table where yellow-throated white orchids, ivy, pale green lichen, and purple statice spill out of a glass vase from the old Braswell's Clothing Store that no longer exists. In a crystal punch bowl, orange slices float in ginger ale punch next to a silver dish piled high with pecan-flavored meringues and pecan puff cookies. The delicate cookies required hours of chopping pecans into a fine meal, mixing the meal with other ingredients, baking, and then rolling the cookies in white sugar, all according to instructions penned in an elegant, faded script more than fifty years ago.

Their president stands, and the women rise from their seats, bow their heads towards the yellow pine floor, and recite in unison the words of the prayer that they, their mothers, and their mothers' mothers have repeated so earnestly for eighty years:

Keep us, O God, from pettiness; let us be large in thought, in word,
and in deed.

Let us be done with fault-finding and leave off self-seeking.

May we never be hasty in judgment and always be generous.

Let us take time for all things, make us to grow calm, serene, and gentle.

Teach us to put into action our better impulses, straight forward and
unafraid.

Grant that we may realize it is the little things that create differences,
that in the big things of life we are as one.

And may we strive to touch and to know the great common human
heart of us all,

And, O Lord God, let us not forget to be kind.

chapter 9:

Brother Jukebox (*Oxford, Mississippi, 1992*)

They brought my daddy's body . . . I remember they brought him in a wagon. He was found in a field there . . . near Santa Fe Station. He was still alive when Aunt Ann's son went down in the field.

This was pioneer days in Florida and [he] was working at a lumber mill temporarily, out from Starke. They had this midnight special that went through Santa Fe [near where] we were living with Grandma Adeline. [Daddy] came home on the weekends to be with Mama and us children and the conductor would stop the train, slow it up as it went through Aunt Ann's field. That time, the regular conductor wasn't on there and the one that was on there wouldn't stop the train. And I think, from what I know of him, I think he jumped and the rear end of the train hurt his back as he jumped.

They said had he lived he would have been a paraplegic from the waist down. Mama went there and he knew her but he died after she got there. I never questioned Mama for too many details. He spoke to her and told her he had some candy for us in his pocket. He remembered that. And I think she told us that to let us know that he did think about us, that he really loved us. He was laid out on boards stretched between two chairs.

The hearse came the night before and it was parked out in front of the house and, of course, the horses to pull it [were put] in stalls at the

barn. But the hearse was parked out in front. It had purple drapes and
I think that's why your mother . . . why Hortense doesn't like purple . . .
where she got that idea.

—Nancy Meggs McWhinnie, May 1988[1]

Aunt Nancy was Mother's younger sister, who envied their father's attentions
to Mother, his firstborn. Inevitably, perhaps, Aunt Nancy and my younger sister
Emily became close friends. Although there is a wealth of unspoken love between
Emily and me, except for brief and widely separated occasions, she and I have
never been close: Emily complains that, when she's around me, she finds out
things she doesn't want to know. No one could ever say that about her, for she is
the soul of restraint. My taciturn Aunt Nancy was childless and, in an emotional
sense, she took my sister.

In August 1991—nine months after an oncologist's grim prediction and
her move to Emily's home in Orlando—Mother was dying. Those nine months
had been a special kind of hell—a blur of migraine headaches and dreams
of Mother lost, falling, or hurt—and me unable to save her. Neither letters,
flowers, nor plane trips helped the tension. We had lived just one block apart for
thirteen years, but now we were separated by a thousand miles and the people who
interpreted us to each other. Mother's handwriting had become a scribble, her
voice a whisper.

A year before, Mother had come to see me in Oxford and, waving one
delicate hand back and forth in the air, demanded a trip "up the Mississippi and
down the Mississippi." In a picture of us on the deck of the Island Queen river
boat, her startling thinness shows. She had shrunk in the six months since I left
home and beside her I was a giantess. In the photograph, we are wearing identical,
cheap, wide-brimmed straw hats and I have on a purple jacket. Mama did hate
purple. "Loud," I can hear her saying. "It sure is loud."

Leaving Oxford for Orlando that hot, August day, I dismissed from my
mind the University of Mississippi and its Center for the Study of Southern
Culture. My apartment and the county courthouse William Faulkner's Benjy

could see only in fragments no longer existed. I passed the entrance to the Natchez Trace and Elvis's shotgun house at Tupelo, and they were nothing to me. Somewhere along the highway between Tupelo and Birmingham, I became indifferent to the road, its unevenness. In my mind, I was already walking up the steps of my sister's home, tapping on the front door for Mother's friend and neighbor from Alachua, Rosemary Bryant, who would come putting one finger

My sister, Emily, and me (right) at the Strickland Fish Camp, Marco Island on the Gulf of Mexico, 1949. From a family album. Used by permission.

My mother, Hortense
Cauthen, and me in Memphis
on the *Island Queen*, 1990.
From a family album. Used
by permission.

to her lips, signalling quiet.[2] I would step over the doorsill, look to the left, and see, turning toward me from behind the shining rails of a hospital bed, Mama's drawn face in a halo of white hair. From beneath the aluminum rails, I would see her blue eyes. I would embrace her again and we would resolve longstanding differences, but first I must drive the distance between us.

In Birmingham, a hard rain obscured detour signs and neon cones on a road under construction and I made a number of wrong turns trying to negotiate the slick, unfamiliar streets. This trip, I thought, is like my life: bumbling, slow, determined. Looking for companionship, I fiddled with the radio dial, remembering a drive along a dirt road in a pickup truck with an Alachua friend who exhorted me to study country music. "It tells the truth," he said. "Just listen to it."

Over the years, I have listened and thoughtfully. In this music, men and women sing jauntily of drunkenness and adulteries, swagger, and wear suggestive smiles. Belligerently, I have sung along with them and, seeing my own face in the rearview mirror, I have sometimes laughed out loud. Driving from Mississippi that night, I tuned in local stations, getting a feel for the people who live along the route. "Don't just sit there and squinch the spirit," a black preacher shouted out, and right behind him on the next station someone sang a haunting song about Hank Williams's ghost.

The most haunting songs of all were about the loss of the Confederacy: Shiloh, Corinth, Vicksburg, Atlanta. In Mississippi, the smoky battlefields of the Civil War are a presence I never felt strongly in Florida. Today's Florida is more international than Southern, changing so rapidly that perhaps it's remarkable that I identify myself as Southern at all. My identification as a Southerner, however, rests neither on tangible evidence like the Cauthen gravestone at Antioch Cemetery lettered "C.S.A. Fl 9th Reg." nor on stories told me by Alachuans like Doris Dansby, whose two grandfathers fought against each other in the Civil War Battle of Olustee. No, this Southerness is attitudinal, an ambivalent stance of willful defiance and stoic compliance—the mutually contradictory legacies of my very different parents. From Daddy I inherited the habit of drawing lines in the sand and, from Mother, an overconcern with other people's opinions. My parents' frontier and Victorian mentalities united, making me Southern at conception.[3]

I did not need to study Sherman's march through Georgia or count the glittering Confederate crosses at Newnansville and Antioch. I did not have to be told that the pied cattle on my grandfather's farm descended from the same gene pool as did the animals caught in the Florida scrub and butchered for the Rebel Army.[4] At my cousin Leon's house in Monteocha, you have to walk past three Confederate flags to get in the back door.

Outside Birmingham, the rain stopped, and I opened the car windows. The cool night air rushed in as a man's voice sang on the radio: "Brother Jukebox/ Sister Wine/Mother Freedom/Father Time." Simultaneously, I caught the scent of freshly dug soil, the earth as it smelled all summer long after my father died. "Brother Jukebox" sounded like the music that blared from my friend's pickup truck as I drank bourbon sitting on Daddy's grave.

Listening to the radio, I passed bridges, roads, and buildings named for George Wallace, Rosa Parks, and Martin Luther King, Jr. These were mere names in newspaper headlines until I learned firsthand from people such as Letha DeCoursey about lynchings and civil rights inside the microcosm of Alachua. In the churches of Gussie Lee and Charles Lawson, I learned how differently African-Americans interpret Christianity and, when Rebecca Wallace trusted me with the treasured family photograph I hung above my bed, I encountered humility. I, too, have come to feel as native daughter Ethel O'Dea must have when, during one of the town forums, she proclaimed, "I feel like the whole town is my family."

In the middle of the night, the road from Birmingham to Montgomery was a nearly deserted straight line along which, every ten minutes, I passed a car with Alabama plates. Alabama decorates its license plate with that most enigmatic of all human organs, a heart. Since before Beowulf left the mead hall, men and women have been telling stories to explain the motives of the heart.

Sometime during the night, my car windshield became that same black field at Santa Fe where, on a cool March night in 1909, a man's body fell from a train. As I drove, I thought about my Aunt Nancy's story: the twisted body, the white-faced young woman who was my grandmother. I saw everything: the man's hand struggling through the damp field grasses toward the candy in his pocket, how his long thin fingers loosened and lay still. It must have seemed to those who were there that, without the sound of his breathing, the field all at once grew quiet.

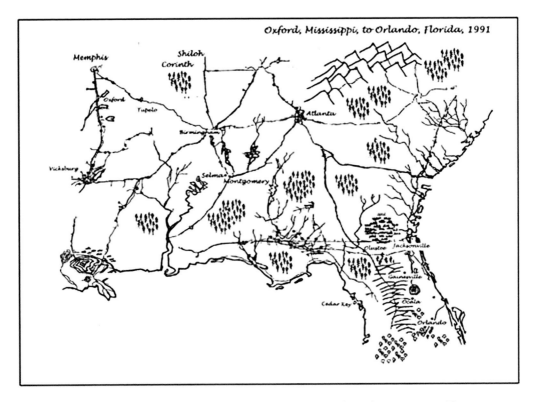

Oxford, Mississippi, to Orlando, Florida, 1991. Map by Hal Cauthen (2006). Used by permission.

"Devastated" is the word Mother used to describe how she felt at age four when her father died—"rendered desolate." He had given her the woven baby doll carriage she pushed about the veranda of her grandmother's house. Over its colored spool trim she looked down at the doll he had brought her.[5] At eighty-six, Mother still spoke of her father as though she was with him yesterday, and it is true that all her life she felt his death as a prolonged abandonment. Some part of Mother did not survive his leaving.

As I drove, I realized that my mother's impending death was only one in a succession of deaths that stretched back beyond her father's and forward past my own. In this context, my grandfather became more than a detail from an oral history or the brown-eyed schoolboy looking out of Grandmother's velvety picture album. Family scenarios played on the windshield in front of me. In them I recognized not only Mama's father, mother, sister, and brother; I recognized the players in my own life as well.

The second time the words of "Brother Jukebox" sounded, I turned up the volume and, steering the car with one hand, jotted lyrics with the other:

> Brother Jukebox, Sister Wine.
> Mother Freedom, Father Time.
> Since she . . . left me . . . by myself,
> You're the on-ly . . . fam-i-ly . . .
> I've got le-eft.
>
> I go down . . . to that same old ca-fe
> Where I try to wash my troub-les a-way.
> I'm still down and I'm all alone,
> but it beats stayin' at home.[6]

This fellow claims a bar has replaced his family. He tells his listeners that his brother and sister are the music he hears and the wine he drinks. I wanted to dismiss as just another country song the catchy tune with its raucous piano tinkling in the background, but it still jangled in my head. Like many others, this song is about the twin refuges of sex and alcohol and the rationalizations of an alcoholic singer. Listening, I saw Daddy again, with a hangover frown on his face.

Alcohol offers one kind of refuge; writing offers another. As I drove with one hand and scratched out notes with the other, I knew that every syllable I put on the page would push me toward this inevitable reckoning: the ordering of write and rewrite. "Bro J, Sis W," I jotted, headed toward the white-domed capitol building in Montgomery.

When I reached Orlando, I went into a music store and bought the tape. "Brother Jukebox, Sister Wine, Mother Freedom, Father Time": everything, I thought, could be talked about under those headings—my father's death; my great-grandfather Doss and the other men of Florida's Ninth Infantry who approached Appomattox together; the past, the future; and Mother's death—they are all connected. In the year since I bought the tape, I have been writing down what comes to mind when I listen to the music I first heard that night.

Brother Jukebox: Daddy's funeral where my beloved uncles, Willie and Orion, stood under the shade of a dogwood tree at Antioch, watching me shovel dirt onto their brother's grave next to my little brother's tiny one.[7] If he had lived, would this baby born before me have been like my father? Or might he have been like Mother's only brother, Colson, who, like the singer of the song, tried to "wash . . . [his] . . . troubles away" with alcohol and ended by shooting himself in an unpainted migrant shack at Santa Fe a mile from where his own father had fallen from a train?

For a year after her brother's funeral, I could hear Mother's sobbing in the night, even in my bedroom at the back of the house. She never wanted to talk about her only brother's suicide, but I needed to. It has haunted me all my life. All during Uncle Colson's graveside funeral service, I sat near the casket with my legs crossed and head bowed. From time to time, I pressed the tip of my high-heeled shoe against the corner of the casket. I wished I could let Uncle Colson know he was not entirely alone. I wished he had not got out of bed that November morning, gone to the closet, come back to sit on the edge of the bed and cock the rifle, then lie down with it.

For me, explanation and understanding require a written process. This process is like going again into North Florida's Bat Cave: dropping through the entrance face down and moving forward, crawling in the dark. On all fours, I am trying to find my way along a path I am marking with words. I am praying to be repaid as I was in the cave, by reaching a place where—if only for a moment—I can see the hanging bodies of small bats, not as ugliness on the cave walls but as the real embellishments they are, drawing light and winking around me like jewels.

The Cauthen farmhouse in Alachua County on US 441, 1983. Photograph by William A. Hunt. Used by permission.

Sister Wine: My younger sister Emily's stern face behind a stemmed glass of red wine. She is beautiful, but has become as remote as Nefertiti. She suffers, she says, from a terrible mistrust because of the lies I told when we were small. Does she mean the time I said I was an alien from another planet who had taken over her body? Does she recall the doll I claimed was a real baby and would not let her hold for weeks?

Were Letha and Rebecca ever so at odds? Aunt Tomye and Huldah? Mary Lou and Vernon, like double yolks in a single egg, have endured and matured together into a gentle old age. Each starts sentences for the other: "Mary Lou thinks we should . . . " "Vernon says we will . . . " They bob their heads in unison, beam twin smiles. They are content. "Sister says . . ," Mary Lou begins, and out of Vernon's mouth drops the rest of the sentence. It is as though they spoke with the same mouth or out of the same heart; and this is why I speak here to my own sister, saying, these are your people, too: Uncle Colson who shot himself, Grandfather Meggs who fell from the train, our mother dying. Therefore:

> out of the parts of me
> that are our mother
> and our father,
> I salute you,
> celebrating us
> even in this condition, for
> in our yet unborn grandchildren
> waits this same ancient
> and ineradicable problem:
> how to love.

Somewhere behind that Nefertiti face is my baby sister who came home from Alachua General Hospital wearing a bracelet of pink beads. One at a time, I pushed at each bead encircling her tiny arm while Mama spelled out the letters of the name I had chosen sitting on the porch between her and Daddy in the summer twilight a month before: Emily. Emily Kathleen.

What is the critical element in attachment? What creates the bonds between biological or spiritual sisters? Vada and I riding old roads bordered by toadflax, Huldah placing a bit of unleavened communion bread on the tip of my tongue, Letha gathering me into her family by telling me of her grandfather, the slave, Brisker Blue—these are the moments sisters have.

Reaching out like human stars, we meet the missing parts of ourselves in other people. Our wounds are actually gifts, the real mouths out of which we speak. And this is true, of course, not only for biological kin, and not only for women.

Mother Freedom: I do not like to dwell on Mother's final moments in Orlando when the very last of her body's cells failed. But I imagine her memories of Alachua County—its distant forests matted like hair against the evenness of cleared fields, the yellow daisies of her kitchen wallpaper, and all the faces she ever loved—coming together at once, like a collage. For a moment, I feel her pulling us close. Then the images soften and lose definition. As fragile as bits of pastel tissue, they fall away and are gone.

Like my father's, her remembered voice—as distinct as a fingerprint, as intricately ridged as the fascinating complications of her personality—will fade. I will have to let go of the mottled brown spots on her thin arms; forget the luminous folds of breast, stomach, and thigh; how the flesh poured itself into pools of liquid pearl as her body was turned in the hospital bed; the innocent transparency of her skin. Mother, in old age, was beautiful. She slept peacefully, a cheek cupped in one hand, her face framed in luxuriant white.

"The only real freedom is peace of mind," Mother said one day, sitting at my sister's glass-topped breakfast table. "I want you to know I see the goal of death as peace."

At one o'clock in the afternoon, the black hearse carrying Mother's body, the limousine which Rosemary and my grown son William and I rode in, Emily's car, and those of friends and relatives pulled away from the funeral home, and drove north on Gainesville's Main Street with their headlights shining. We passed the Alachua County Courthouse Square where Cauthen family marriages, births, deaths, sales and purchases of land have been recorded for nearly 200 years. Courthouse documents show that William married Celia in 1859; that Frank served as a deputy sheriff in the early 1900s; and that the names of seven of Celia's grandchildren were Marcus, Ira, Clyatt, Orion, Allen, Willie, and Nadine. On the surreal streets bordering the square, pedestrians crossed eating sandwiches, thinking perhaps of desultory love affairs, returning to their earnest work.

The line of cars did not proceed directly to the cemetery, but north-northwest, towards Alachua. Mother had wished hopelessly to come home and say goodbye, but had not been allowed to do so. Led by the hearse bearing her body, our cortege traveled a route I like to think she might have chosen, up the winding Millhopper Road through San Felasco Hammock.

The back of our farm bordered San Felasco and, when I was a child, Daddy told me that bears and panthers were still there. Millhopper Road gets its name from the story told of an Indian princess stolen by the devil during the night. Roused by her cries, stalwart Indian braves gave chase. To escape, the devil stomped his foot and created the sinkhole called Devil's Millhopper through which he disappeared, carrying the princess. The streams that trickle down the walls of the sink are the tears of the Indian maiden's people, still crying for her release.[8]

Millhopper Road intersects Shaw Memorial Highway, and soon we passed a subdivision of single-family homes that have sprung up where I once picked summer corn on Conye Shaw's enormous family farm. We turned north, passing Mt. Nebo Church where Alex Lundy's father is buried and the Mobley farm where the DeCoursey family cropped shares. We entered Alachua on Church Street and turned left at the First Baptist Church.

First Baptist was my grandparents' church and Mother's. My sister and father and I were also baptized there. For me, First Baptist represents Vacation Bible School's grape juice and sugar cookies juxtaposed with warnings of "eternal

(Left to right) Hortense, Colson, and Nancy Meggs, ca. 1917. From a family album. Used by permission.

damnation in hell." During the Depression, Mother taught school in the church's cold downstairs basement while, at the top of the hill above Church Street, WPA workers built an addition to Alachua High School.

We followed the hearse to Mother's house in Alachua, purchased after the farm was sold when Daddy was too ill to work it, and passed near where the old railroad station once stood at the south end of Main Street. Here, the young children, Hortense, Nancy, and Colson, hung over the shoulders of a telegrapher taking down messages that arrived in cryptic dots and dashes from the outside world.

Mother grew up in town. From behind the limousine's darkened windows, I imagined her there again, walking past Warner Mott's blacksmith shop where she "liked to hear the ringing of the metal." I saw her nod to the old men at the barbershop who she said "chewed tobacco and spit it all over the place." She went past the drowsing mules at DeWitt Hague's Stable and up Church Street where once, in winter, her grocery sack broke and apples rolled behind her down the hill, almost as far as the Methodist Church. Mother collected the apples into her pulled-up skirts and marched home to her severe stepfather, Malachi Strickland, with her underwear exposed.

I can see the children: eating apples, roasting oysters, drawing water in pails from the cistern for my grandmother, and playing at being Indians in the coffee weed field. One day in Orlando, after winning at cards, Mother quoted whole poems to her nurses and several stanzas of "The Song of Hiawatha":

> By the shores of Gitche Gumee,
> By the shining Big-Sea-Water,
> Stood the wigwam of Nokomis,
> Daughter of the moon . . . .[9]

Evidently this poem learned in grade school furnished inspiration for the children's play, for Mother followed her one-stanza recital with this:

There was Hortense and Nancy and Colson and Kenneth and William Bennett, and Lucile Ellis. We played in the field next door to my parents' house, in the coffee weeds. The coffee weeds that we pulled up and used to build our "wigwams" were taller than we were. We tied them up by the roots at the top with string or, if we did not have string, we twisted smaller weeds around them to hold them tight. Coffee weeds are tall, strong weeds and we made the wigwams [so they reached] up over our heads and [we] bowed our heads to get in so we wouldn't knock the top off. We had a lot of imagination.

We got the idea at school. We dug in the dirt and played Indian. Got us a piece of bacon out of the storehouse and stuck sticks in the ground so that they leaned over the fire so we could toast the bacon. Our parents didn't know it.

Colson built the fire, but we all had a say-so in things. We were squaws and Indian chiefs sitting around that fire, telling make-believe stories.

Our field was bordered on two sides by roads. One was really just a path people walked through the woods to the school. The other— Church Street—was all sand. There was a hickory tree by the fence and we used to climb to the top of it and look down on the town. Whoever was up there would tell the other younguns that a car was coming or a man on a horse or a wagon with cotton.[10]

The children who played at being Indians in the coffee weeds acted out an old Alachua story; they had heard about the Seminole Wars. They knew nothing, however, of the area's earlier inhabitants, the Timucuans. They had not seen artist Jacques LeMoyne's sixteenth-century depictions of a muscular race of stately men and women who wore more tattoos than clothing and slept, not in wigwams, but on raised platforms in the smoke of smudge fires built to discourage insects.[11] The children had no conception of Potano Woman, just miles away who, already, had lain for 400 years with her arms crossed over her chest.

Our slow-moving hearse, limousine, and line of cars left Mother's childhood home and went back down the hill past the modern-day businesses that have replaced Field's Store where the Greyhound bus once stopped and where, as schoolchildren, my friends and I unwrapped Mary Jane candies from waxy yellow papers; past the old ice plant where Mother said whole turkeys stayed frozen in individual blocks of ice for years; and out US 441, towards Hague. When we passed the farm Mama and Daddy sold in 1973, yellow fires flashed in our old hickories at the foot of the driveway. It was November, the end of the year.

About Freedom: Mother is released, loosed from the cares of this earth, from the horror of her father and Colson's deaths, her mother's, stepfather's; from her beautiful boy-child born dead; from uncle, husband, friend—their funerals she saw to. The minister, the funeral home, what to dress the body in, casket open/casket closed, flowers, food . . . the endless returning of dishes the food came in, the writing of notes: these necessities, she is done with. Released now from form, she will not have to mark off another friend's name in her address book.

And so she is freed. Mother is free of twenty-four hours a day, 365 days a year, and income tax time. She is no longer subject to the successive betrayals of the body. She is not concerned with the interest rates on certificates of deposit or what Foevrin Power and his cronies will decide for Alachua tomorrow. She will not be perturbed if the air conditioning fails.

Unfastened from the mundane grip of this world, Mother has moved on to tea parties more elaborate than the earthly ones she loved—in the galaxies, to music that orchestrates the earth's turning. Close-up, she examines the stars. Moving more easily than she did here, she finds the new place even more familiar than the winged rocking chair in which she crooned my sister and me to sleep before our winter fireplace in the farmhouse of our youth.

Father Time: Since my father's death, I have been collecting with a tape recorder the scattered fragments of Alachua's story in what are called "oral histories" and transcribing them into written documents. Transcripts, however, cannot replace the actuality of the individuals who have given me the pieces of Alachua I am trying to fit into one mosaic, the aural enchantment of language from whole worlds vanished, the scowls and guffaws accompanying the tellings, the forehead wrinklings and poundings of fists on tabletops. The ghosts of the storytellers and the ghosts of those others they described are more substantive to me than the ordinary people who today walk Alachua's streets.

Because for me the past is real, the young McFadden sisters still pose in Dr. Bishop's front porch cupola for a photographer; there they are, their corkscrew curls not yet in sepia; the whole twentieth century stretched out like a clear, shining path before their eyes. Down a dirt Main Street walk the pubescent girls, Letha and Rebecca, each holding a handle of the galvanized metal tub filled with the dishes they sell door-to-door. A small boy named Emery Williams pedals his tricycle southward, towards the whistle of a train at the railway depot.

At some distance from the little town that has only recently been incorporated, Huldah and Tomye, still just babies, play in the shade of an oak tree not far from where Potano Woman lies. To the east at Santa Fe and Monteocha, the Doke, Cauthen, Cellon, and Dampier families clear trees from the land their children will help them farm. At my great-grandmother Adeline's farm, two little girls named Hortense and Nancy take turns feeding their baby brother, Colson. The children's father works at Starke and will come home tomorrow on the midnight train.

Death has forced into my vocabulary "before Mother died" and "after Mother died." Both what we know of her—and her understanding of the town—have become story. With the deaths of our oldest storytellers, more than a century's worth of detail blurs, slips from view, and becomes the past.

The words "past," "present," "before," and "after" are linear markers that attempt to compartmentalize experience. They are necessary; using them releases me to a present no longer held hostage by the past. To arrive at now, I not only physically had to leave Alachua, but also to achieve a mental distance. I had to write all of this down.

132

I write, encouraged by a crowd of invisible witnesses; like you, I am bound to them by the planet we imperil and the common denominator of the grave. And I am also bound by story. I know I am nearly done with this one when I dream, as I did last night, of wallpaper peeling in furious strips from those familiar walls in the Alachua house which was once my home. I know it as Alachua recedes and I must look back over my shoulder to see her deceptively disparate people, haunted yet by the perplexing fact that, even in ancient Africa, black was considered evil and white, good.[12]

Fastened by my parents' lives and those of our ancestors whose ashes compose that venerable soil, I am forever wedded to place. Indisputably, I am marked by conflicting allegiances to the country in my father and the town in my mother. My family is the land, Victorianism, alcoholism, evangelicalism, fire and damnation, all as sweet to me as the dark ribbon of cane syrup Grandmother Cauthen poured into my clabber bowl at her kitchen table on the Monteocha farm.

About Time: Freedom and peace are achieved in the moment. We are free only when we stand in the clarifying instant, examining its lineaments. In this present little instant where I stand, it is acceptable to be a solitary woman of forty-nine, ignoring, perhaps foolishly, the world's usual expectations in order to write these messages about wanting more than I will ever get. This morning I know with surety that nothing will ever be richer than this moment in which I sit scrawling words at high noon on a Sunday when the yellow forsythia blooms in full sun beyond my red car, the purple irises begin to droop, as is natural, and the bits of oatmeal dry in my blue morning bowl.

The stern necessity for placing myself in relation to the events of my life is what brought me to Mississippi and softened my ambivalence toward Alachua. My parents, of course, had fastened me there: Mother on a farm, but always wanting to return to town; Daddy caring not a jot for town ways, wanting for himself only another cow or the money to buy one.

She embodied the Victorian thinking
of the town, and honored its rules;
and he, country all through,
was gentleman enough
to charm women and children,
knew the town's rules
and did not honor them.
For her, proper place settings
and Sunday School
were necessities.
If a piece of fence was loose
or a pig gone missing,
he ate her biscuits cold
from the back of the stove.
She, finding him untameable,
and he, finding her incorruptible,
both suffered; but stayed.
My parents:
the country, the town.

PART THREE:
THIS PLACE, ALACHUA

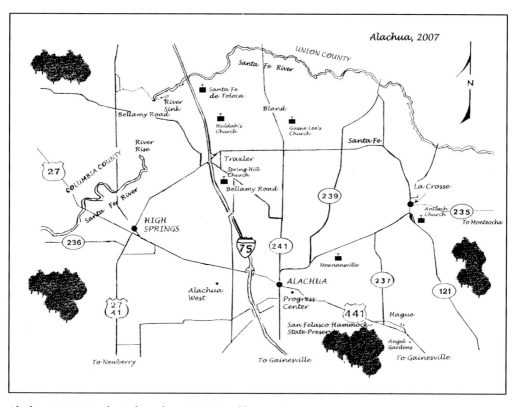

Alachua, 2007. Map by Hal Cauthen (2007). Used by permission.

From Angel to Harmony Gardens (*Alachua, Florida, 2007*)

> Detroit was once a town like Alachua, a little old tiny village
> with people and churches scattered around.
>
> —Jim Kelly, 1983[1]

Two days past Mother's funeral in 1991, my cousin Leon drove his truck
with rifles hanging in its back window to Antioch Cemetery, stepped out, opened a
cooler in the truck bed, and took out two beers. He flipped the caps and handed me
one of the cans. Leon inherited his father's—my Uncle Orion's—predisposition
for reflection. He's also learned a succinctness I haven't. We talked about our
loves; other than a dozen living souls, the people Leon cares most about are all
underground. I asked what was dearest to him.

"My place," he said instantly, meaning the seventeen acres left of the entire
section that once belonged to our great-grandfather.[2] "Then my mama and daddy,"
he continued, for they were still living. "My children . . . and these here," he said,
stirring the air in front of our Cauthen grandparents' pink marble headstones with
the hand holding his beer. "These here," he repeated, "and then you'd be coming
into view." He had named the land first.

I realize that not all farmers respect the land in its own right, that some regard
it as only a commodity translatable into dollars. But Leon loves it just because
it is, for itself, because it is the land. I stood there in the cemetery, thinking
about humankind's either/or tendency, its weakness for us/them thinking. I was
wondering why I have so few people to discuss this with.

We don't like probing our belief systems; unquestioned, they give us stability and quiet of mind. Mother, coming home from church one day, fretted over her own biblical interpretation of a particular scripture; it didn't jibe with those of her friends at church. How ironic that we struggle to conform our thinking, in order to belong, and that very conformity then puts us at odds with other groups. Isn't it reasonable to assume that, just as a book or a movie is interpreted differently by individuals and as surely as no two friendships are duplicates, none of us knows God in quite the same manner as does our neighbor?

Once, even the spirits of trees were honored, a novel idea to those who dismiss them as inanimate, not knowing that their molecules, as well as those in the plywood desktop on which I write each day, derive from one source and are living entities. Recently, I've been reading about humankind's conception of itself as separate from nature, how that way of seeing ourselves accounts for our distancing from, and destruction of, the natural world.[3]

Whether you think global warming is a joke or can't quite grasp why it should matter that we no longer have a dusky seaside sparrow, it's clear we're using up the world's resources, faster and faster. I didn't say any of this to Leon.

We stood there together until, unexpectedly, Leon spoke. "Some people...," he observed slowly, as though the thought had just occurred to him, "some people gone and got educated beyond their intelligence."

Since I left for Mississippi in 1990, the City of Alachua has sprawled along US 441 in three directions: north, two miles beyond I-75; south, toward Gainesville; and west, spilling out into the countryside off CR 235-A. *Gainesville Sun* stories, such as "Alachua's Choice: Small Town or Boom Town," suggest that huge change looms, yet prominently displayed road signs still read "Florida's Rural City, 1995." In spite of feeling I've already achieved perspective on this place, yesterday I drove fifty miles south of where I now live in White Springs, going "home" to find out if it still feels the same.

Zoning and development decisions concerning the area where a Dollar General located its new warehouse west of town have provoked an uproar, and the commission that forever and ever had been white and male has a new balance: in early 2007, three men and two women, three whites and two blacks. According to the *Gainesville Sun*, two of the new commissioners have strong reservations about a "progress" they see as profiting only a few while stealing Alachua's rural quiet, unsettling not only old-timers, but also the newcomers who were drawn here by the town's "left behind" feel.

North Main Street is still a black residential area, but, as I drove past the once-abandoned theater shell on middle Main Street, I glimpsed two women inside. They were wearing sundresses and unwrapping sandwiches on benches shaded by Kool-Aid-pink crape myrtles. The curvilinear street was jammed with the cars of lunch customers at Conestogas Restaurant.

Squeezed together on I-75 are the same fast food stops travelers have come to expect at interstate exits across America. When I stepped into Alachua's Waffle House, I had never before seen blacks in there. While I, a white-haired woman in overalls, waited at the counter for my eggs, bacon, and grits, one booth emptied. A solitary black man slid into it.

Beside me, a fiftyish white man was describing the prison term he'd just completed; he was going back to the job he had "before they arrested me." Two teenage males, tattooed from shoulders to wrists, were rapt. Everyone but me was smoking, as though that Saturday was the last day for cigarettes. I gulped the food, washed down Tylenol Sinus with coffee, and got back in my car.

Nearly thirteen years ago, on the day I returned to Alachua after completing graduate school at the University of Mississippi, I barreled down the I-75 exit ramp (which deposited me in Alachua, on US 441, two miles south of its northernmost city limits sign) towards a large billboard advertising a place down the road called "Angel Gardens," a New Age enterprise housed in a spacious turn-of-the-twentieth-century house wrapped with porches, its lawn hidden under thousands of pieces of concrete lawn statuary: pigs, snails, Bo Peeps, gargoyles, and, of course, angels. I thought the billboard curious, and, later, for personal reasons, I found Angel Gardens just plain strange. On my most recent visit, I left I-75 and headed south on US 441, passing the familiar franchises that constitute what James Howard Kunstler calls a "geography of nowhere."[4]

In the four-laned 441 median, the live oaks and magnolias planted the year I left looked robust, which made me wonder why the Florida Department of Transportation's cutting of the original sixty-year-old trees in 1988 had so distressed me. Because of tradition; also, as I recall, contrary to DOT claims, not all the trees were diseased. Aunt Tomye, too, had been so upset she left a message on my answering machine, threatening to tie herself to one of the trees in front of her house.

On 441, half of the commuter traffic is pickup trucks driven by men and women (and their grown children) who have had to quit family farms and take office jobs in Gainesville in order to pay the taxes on their dormant fields. In the fifteen miles between the I-75 exit where I entered Alachua on the north and its southern city limits sign, two areas remain unscarred. Opposite Aunt Tomye and Uncle Willie's old home—now headquarters for a professional waste collection company—lies the place known to only a few oldtimers as "Itchibottom," a low spot that thickens in spring with white blooms, then briefly glistens silver during April's rains. Itchibottom appeared unchanged, except that a realtor's sign stood in front. Until quite recently, the wide green fields of my daddy's farm were also unchanged; now they are planted in pines.

In 1995, the farmhouse I grew up in was given away by the property's current owner. The house was moved south to Angel Gardens and set next to the spacious house with porches, but further back from the road. Over the phone the proprietress told me, "You'll love it. You'll want to write something about growing up in the house and how it became the Angel Gardens Cafe." She added that she had friends who were clairvoyant and audiovoyant. They could see and hear all that had taken place in our former home.

Several times since the farm was sold in 1973, I had impulsively turned my car up the half-circle of driveway I once rode on the running board of my father's pickup, on a bicycle with training wheels, and astride my horse, Prince, looping in figure eights around Mother's flower beds. With each visit, I relived three years of walking across the lawn and up the front steps, my eyes fixed on the window of the room where my father lay, surrounded by oxygen tanks and medicine bottles. However painful, the memories the house held were mine, its rooms private repositories of images I could examine whenever I had nerve enough.

In 1995, crossing the wide porch of the new cafe at Angel Gardens for the first time also required nerve. Here, my parents and sister and I had rocked in handmade chairs while summer suns set; mornings in August, Granddaddy Strickland crowded the entrance with silver pails of freshly picked figs for Mother to can, along with tomatoes, squash, okra, and corn: all these my mother cooked and poured into sterilized Mason jars she sealed with rubber rings and capped. Here Daddy sat on Saturday nights, telling stories, cigarette in one hand, a bottle of Red

My father, Allen Cauthen, and me on the steps of our home in the country, 1947, when I was four years old. From a family album. Used by permission.

My father and me at our farm, ca. 1948. From a family album. Used by permission.

Cap ale in the other. After midday Sunday dinners, he often teased us through long afternoons, declaring that each approaching car on 441 held "Aunt Nadine, come all the way from Nokomis. There she is now, slowing down, gonna pull on in the driveway." When Daddy's older brother, Uncle Clyatt, visited, he paid Emily and me a penny for each minute we could "sit still and let the grown-ups talk."

These images of family vaporized at once when I visited the house in its changed setting. I parked my car, wound my way through the statuary, and climbed the house's new, wider steps, which I found busy with the play of children and the hurdy-gurdy music of two recently installed carousels. Inside, in what used to be the doorway to my parents' bedroom, I stepped past a tall, thin waiter. Behind him, where my parents lay together for more than thirty years, four heavily made-up matrons were clinking teacups painted with the faces of angels.

Did I want the Watercress Sandwich at $6.98 or the Cream of Lentil Soup at $6.98? Chips with both. I felt dizzy as, over the top edge of the menu, I scrutinized the entrance I'd just come through. The cafe was not one room, but several alcoves, each opening onto the next, all decorated with angels—lamps, paintings, wall hangings of cow angels, bunny angels, and even angel rocks. Around me hung comical Disney characters with wings. In the alcove created out of the bedroom where I slept for twenty years, two lovers—she, wearing neon rings on her fingers, and he, bespectacled and earnest—surrounded by Sistine Chapel wallpaper were happily cracking open imitation crab legs made of plastic to get at the soy stuffing inside. God and Adam's hands swung from a mobile above the couple's heads. At the elbow of the man exuberantly attacking his soy crab was the windowsill where on hot summer nights I lay my head and fell asleep, listening to Prince as he snorted and thundered through the barnyard.

On the reverse side of the cafe's "Menu for the Millennium," an advertisement read, "Love Master Mission Class. Advanced Energy Healing, Astral Projection. What to do after Kundalini awakens." While I was reading this, ordinary-looking people went in and out of the front door, tramping over the exact spot where Santa left my sister and me oranges, skates, and matching pink bathrobes quilted in a Cinderella print. I studied each person who entered, wondering which ones were audiovoyant or clairvoyant.

Behind me, the breathy voices of two young women:

"I think my great-grandfather was actually my father."
"You mean, he . . .?"
"Yes. I wish I could talk with him."
"He's dead though, isn't he?"
"He did die, but he's a four-year-old Tibetan boy now. Reincarnated."
"Wow! I'm glad we took that class together."
"Me, too, or I wouldn't know the truth."
"And I wouldn't have remembered Jack and me being knights together at
    King Arthur's Round Table."
"What did Jack say when you told him?"

I didn't catch what Jack had said. The diamond my father gave Mother in 1941 winked on my hand, throwing lights into the room, and I found myself listening for Mother's voice, expecting a pronouncement like the one after she watched a movie about aliens, shortly before her death. "Well," she exclaimed, as the credits rolled, "if that's not the silliest thing I ever saw."

I have a friend who tells me benign aliens are collecting samples of Earth's flora and fauna, preserving them until our planet's inhabitants are in the mood to think about restoration. I thought of this on that recent day when I drove south toward Angel Gardens while listening to a radio commentator describe the Kissimmee River Restoration Project and the 1994 Everglades Forever Act, both of which, along with Lake Okeechobee, are crucial to the state's water supply. Everglades Forever was supposed to clean up the "river of grass" by 2006, but Governor Jeb Bush signed a bill that "allows the use of moderating provisions in the water quality standards," thereby delaying aspects of the cleanup by ten years. And there have been many predictions that global warming's glacier melts and the expected subsequent rise in sea level mean a major portion of the Everglades might be underwater in another fifty years, within my granddaughter's lifetime.[5]

Just south of Alachua I passed Progress Corporate Park, a research park established in the late 1980s. Its original 130,000 square feet have grown to 360,000, multi-storied buildings are going up, transplanted palm trees put in place, and 700 people report here for work; across the highway sits a new State of Florida regional office, a used auto sales lot, a mini-storage, and on and on—dozens of buildings eradicating natural North Florida, replacing it with a landscape like that of the Detroit characterized by Jim Kelly who, during our town hall meetings, cautioned:

> We could become another Detroit. When they were growing, they let
> their values get completely out of hand. Instead of their values being
> love, joy, and peace, their values got to be big industry, high-paying
> jobs, lots of money, and lots of prestige.[6]

I slowed the car as I approached Angel Gardens's main building, the house with deep porches and several fireplaces that, the first time I saw it, featured a gift shop and a vegetarian grocery. Since my 1995 visit, the eatery housed in our family's simpler dwelling, then named Daniella's and painted lime green and hot pink, had changed its fare, offering expensive wines along with fine Italian dishes; the last time I was there, under the new name Le Papillon, the house was booked for weddings and parties, and dancers cavorted over the exact spot where I imagine myself to have been conceived. Last week I learned that the old Angel Gardens property has been sold, and the grounds are now called Harmony Gardens.

Harmony Gardens is just beyond Alachua's southernmost city limits, Gainesville only ten miles further. I turned back to Hague, once a railway departure point for potato crops, but only notable in my lifetime for its two old churches and a tiny store where farm workers hoping for employment gathered on weekdays at dawn. Most of what came to mind as I traveled through Hague no longer exists; much of it I would not know, except for the writings of observers with sensibilities as different as those of William Bartram, Marjory Stoneman

Douglas, and Jacques LeMoyne whose work allows us to measure today's tinseled Florida against the original, the real. How else would I have glimpsed—behind the RV sales lot at Hague—the nearly mythological and gorgeous shapes of Florida's aboriginal Timucuans, bent over, sowing seed?

Seeking the familiar, I followed CR 237 into the countryside, in the direction of LaCrosse, passing the Cellon Oak, one of the state's two largest live oak trees (*Quercus virginiana*), a remnant of what Bartram commemorated in the late 1700s when he wrote, "the Indians obtain from it a sweet oil, which they use in the cooking of hommony [sic], rice, &c.; and they also roast it in hot embers, eating it as we do chestnuts."[7]

At the newly labeled NW 156th Avenue intersection I am amazed to see that Dampier's Store, where Uncle Willie and I often interrupted our country drives for Cokes and cheese crackers, has vanished. The store closed a few years back; it had been there forever. Each time we drew near it, Uncle Willie declared that, when he was a young boy in the early 1900s, this was the exact corner where the rural mail carrier switched his hot, wet horse for a fresh one. I rambled northwest, then toward the Santa Fe River, passing the Greater New Hope Missionary Baptist Church in which, a lifetime ago, I clapped and swayed while Gussie Lee's piano carved whole phrases in the air.

I found the river, dry and weedy; nearby, Potano Woman rests, invisible beneath a planted field. In this area, subdivisions and realtors' signs abound, mobile homes are fitted tightly between oak trees, and dozens of shiny mailboxes cluster at the entrances to anonymous dirt roads. The road I took that long-ago Sunday morning to help Huldah bake communion bread has been paved, lined on both sides with costly houses that sit well back from the road, unrelated to one another by architecture, plantings, or fences. Not a pasture was left, so I was glad to see Huldah's pecan tree and the bitter-smelling orange and yellow "umbelliferous tufts" of the Lantana, noted by Bartram, flourishing yet.[8]

When I was a girl, nearby High Springs celebrated an annual Tobacco Festival replete with beauty queens in long Chevy convertibles, but on last summer's drive I saw only two fields of tobacco. Like cotton, peanuts, and soybeans, another of the American South's money crops has disappeared. The tobacco auction system was replaced by contracts between tobacco companies and individual farmers, but a 2004 buyout eliminates government price supports and, ultimately, the tobacco industry will get its tobacco wherever it's cheapest, probably overseas.[9] Big Dollar, Tommy Malphurs's tobacco auction barn in High Springs, no longer exists.

Years ago, some prescient property owner nailed up a sign along one of Alachua's dirt roads that reads, "Go Back! Save Yourself! Florida is Dying!" Certainly the Florida I have loved is perishing: Mary Lou, Vernon, Lemon Washington, Pink Frazier, Mattie Richardson, Huldah, Mrs. Traxler, Letha, Chester; they, and many others, are gone. Traxler's cotton gin and the commissary where Letha savored her penny cookie have disappeared from a landscape characterized by "development" and "progress." The countryside has been sliced by realtors into pieces; there is no more countryside.

I headed back into the city, passing my Strickland grandparents' Victorian house where I was pleased to see that someone had repaired the sagging roof under which Granddaddy Strickland regularly reclined on the porch swing, reading his *Bible* after lunch. The trim on the wide window, through which my mother once took note of horse-and-buggy traffic, looked freshly painted.

One afternoon, Vada and I drove out CR 235-A, and I soon understood why one resident said the Dollar General facility serving two states and 600 stores was the largest building she'd ever seen. Vada and I drove and drove and drove, and still we were passing in front of that one structure which looked as if, turned on end, its one million square feet might be as high as Cape Kennedy's Vertical Assembly Building. The city granted Dollar General (DG) money needed for infrastructure, thereby paving the way for further development, such as the Wal-Mart Distribution Center that opened only weeks ago, in March of this year, and SYSCO FOODS, which has purchased property for a redistribution center.

Nearby residents complain about twenty-four-hour-a-day traffic and bright lights that keep them awake, that the beeping of DG's loading and docking trolleys has replaced the music of cicadas and frogs. Dollar General is just the beginning; in its entirety, the proposed development is a $539,000,000 industrial, business, and residential undertaking that some say could double the city's population in thirteen years. Objectors are vociferous; in fact, a few are vulgar. My stack of local newspapers details a long and fractious argument between the older leaders of the community and the Alachua Leadership Alliance whose Website argues against a proposed Wal-Mart Super Center to be built over an underground river, a project objected to even by residents of nearby High Springs concerned about their water quality. Alachua's present city manager, Clovis Watson—who grew up in an Alachua subsidized housing project—is a passionate spokesperson for, and defender of, the city. Watson dismisses critics: "We had 10,000 people at our city's 100th anniversary celebration in 2005! Look at the resources, not the debt, and Dollar General contributes more than $1,000,000 in taxes each year." Watson praises an Alachua that offered him—an African-American former policeman and state body-building champion—the opportunity to rise to the position of city manager. "Coming to work," he says, "is my love."[10]

One businessman told me that, although he often sympathizes with questions raised by those who oppose new development, he does not publicly voice his feelings because he doesn't want to be associated with the "vocal, misguided, and rude" behavior of the opposition. The allegation most reminiscent of Alachua in the 1980s is one charging that government officials themselves have a financial interest in what happens along 235-A.

An estimated doubling of traffic means only a few more paved strips on a peninsula already so veined with roads that, in 2000, Florida taxpayers voted to finance a monorail connecting the state's five largest cities. (They reversed that vote in 2004.) The city's debt, which has more than doubled since 1990, perturbs critics who oppose the city's borrowing of monies for infrastructure designed to lure new businesses. Yet, as Watson pointed out to me, how else can the city attract businesses that create jobs for its growing population? In a state tortured by years of drought and forest fires, then by flooding, followed by heavy rains and, in 2004, by four hurricanes in six weeks, environmentalists gained power at the county level and strictly limited growth in nearby Gainesville, the county seat. I'm told that, in recent elections, the county commission has achieved a more business-friendly makeup and now turns away fewer applicants.

The town and country I described in the first two parts of this book comprise a microcosm of the American South whose old-timers valued even the worn scraps of their grandmothers' quilts and rejoiced in relating their handed-down stories. Present-day Alachua is the New South and a microcosm of a decidedly different sort. Most of what I examined so minutely is gone.

North Florida, which hardly anyone realizes was Southern in its pioneer beginnings and the third state to secede from the Union, was once depicted as Edenic by writers, including the Reverend Elvy Callaway who (in a conversation recounted by writer Gloria Jahoda) insisted that the branchings of the Appalachicola River and the presence of gopherwood trees at Torreya State Park in the Panhandle mark Adam and Eve's original home. Bartram, describing his exploration of the Alachua Savanna (now called Payne's Prairie), says:

> Passing through a great extent of ancient Indian fields, now grown over
> with forests of stately trees, Orange groves, and luxuriant herbage…It
> was the ancient Alachua, the capital of that famous and powerful tribe,
> who peopled the hills surrounding the savanna, when, in days of old,
> they could assemble by thousands at ball play and other juvenile diversions
> and athletic exercises, over those, then happy fields and green plains.[11]

Our gorgeous plains have attracted so many visitors and new residents that now the viability of Florida's fabulous waters is questioned. What of the possibility that heavily populated South Florida, having ruined its own water supply and having larger representation in the state legislature, will take North Florida's? With its inducements to developers such as Disney in the 1970s (including exemption from land-use laws), Florida's legislature imperiled the delicately balanced ecosystem. The state's 1990 population was 13,000,000; the 2000 census records 15,982,378, and, according to the University of Florida's 2004 *Estimates of Population* released in late 2005, Florida's population currently increases at the rate of 368,109 people per year or more than 1,008.5 per day.

The elementary school population in Alachua dropped from 1,029 in 2006 to 984 in 2007, but the schools expect rising figures as the general population increases, drawn by new jobs such as those that SYSCO FOODS will bring when its redistribution warehouse, now under construction, begins hiring.

On Main Street, the most impressive of the town's mansions, Miss Blanche LeRoy's three-story house with fish-scale shingles and Belgian tiles, belongs now to a local Hare Krishna member who once advertised the house as Govinda's Restaurant. This vegetarian eatery was open to the public for only a short time, was then rented out for special occasions, and is now for sale. Miss LeRoy kept her wide porch so bare that you counted not only the high steps mounting to it, but also each board crossed until you stood, finally, at a front door so plain and anonymous, looking so unused, that it might have been permanently sealed. The new owner installed palm trees from street to porch, decked the exterior with hanging baskets of flowers and neon lights, and landscaped Miss LeRoy's broad side yards into immaculate miniature parks. Govinda's advertised a cybercafe. Around back, where a railroad spur once carried cotton, construction workers hammered on a huge addition.

An I-75 billboard north of the city advises "Chant and Be Happy" and advertises tours and food at Alachua's Hare Krishna Temple, located not far from my friend Vada's house. The Dr. Bishop House, where Mary Lou and Vernon posed for photographs 100 years ago, also belongs to the Krishnas, as does a two-story 1920s cottage. Briefly, a Krishna-run gift shop replaced Dr. Joe Thigpen's Drug Store, at the corner of Main Street and Florida Avenue, where my classmates and I once slid dimes over a marble countertop for Coke floats we drank at the drug store's ice cream tables after school. The new shop sold silver jewelry, uncut amber from the Dominican Republic with insects caught whole in its gold, soft Indian dresses, and glossy furniture detailed with elephants, dragons, and wizards. Until recently, a full suit of armor stood out on the sidewalk. The old downtown area is changing again; years ago, some predicted it will end up like neighboring High Springs, a tourist destination advertising antiques and boutiques.

Almost everything is different: members of the Lions Club no longer meet in the chinked log house (where as a school girl I innocently performed black dialect readings) but in a new concrete building that stands next to a Family Dollar store. Opposite the city park, Jimmy Swick's cow pasture has metamorphosed into the red brick of the new Alachua Town Center, a shopping area with greater square footage than all of downtown's shops put together. Its 1,700 acres front on US 441, and additional new growth glimmers along the highway in the direction of I-75. Some established businesses, such as Hitchcock's Foodway—which in my memory had already moved three times—have relocated just beyond the Town Center. Even a nearby Indian mound has been paved over for a parking lot.

Each time I pass through Alachua, headed towards Gainesville on 441, I see that, beyond the Town Center, more buildings have sprung up. Like the colored crystals my sister Emily and I dropped into our aquarium that grew into castles before our eyes, the spectacle of Alachua's growth seems surreal. One day I walked old Main Street alone, stopped in a gift shop, and chatted with its owner. I recognized almost nothing, and Uncle Willie's barber pole was missing. After thanking the shop keeper for the visit, I started toward the door, and the woman said to me, "And where do you come from?"

Off-road, I find that much of the growth is impressive: a new, two-story City Hall, lavish plantings of palms and flowering pear trees, additions to the library, part of the old city admitted to the National Register of Historic Places, the women's club rewrite of its by-laws to include non-whites as members and the handsome renovation of the fieldstone clubhouse itself, these signify a new Alachua. A gated hilltop community of sixty homes on large lots, trees, underground utilities, and private roads, three-story apartment buildings, and a local attorney who vied for the Democratic gubernatorial nomination last year all suggest a new importance and a new pride of place. In February, Alachua's drinking water won a taste test in a regional competition. I chasten myself for thinking negatively and am glad that the 1980s face of Alachua with its boarded-up buildings and small thinking appears to have been replaced by so handsome and striking a visage. The March 30, 2007, edition of the *High Springs Herald* details Alachua's plan for a wildlife corridor linking Progress Corporate Park to San Felasco Hammock, a path through mesic hammock along which rabbits, coyotes, foxes, bobcats, and deer can safely travel.

Although I am no longer a resident and don't have in-depth information about contemporary affairs here, it is good that at last I can look at this town and feel hopeful, for scrutinizing Alachua has always been my way of examining the world, and everywhere I find we are in the grip of an ideology that seems to oppose our survival. Deep in our hearts we all know the earth is imperiled. The current debates over Alachua's growth echo a much larger question: what is humankind's place in the scheme of things?

I will die without knowing the answer to this or the resolutions to many other crucial issues. It's possible these past seventeen years, many of them spent pursuing graduate studies in Mississippi and Florida, have not only destabilized my own belief system, but also entirely alienated me from Alachuans. I hope not; I hope we can come to see—and that I can persist in believing—that we are all one, that we are whole and must give up seeing ourselves as separate, different, and disconnected. Long before the continents broke apart, before this planet had a crust or a moon, we were one. We still are, and our separation from the earth will not be healed until we embrace our true connectedness, for we are, each of us, small and glorious bits in one endless web of being.

On my desk this morning, I am laying out the contents of several plastic bags. These are objects I gathered on the day of my lunch at Angel Gardens, twelve years ago. I had left the restaurant, driven my favorite dirt roads for comfort, and, finally, turned back onto US 441. Headed north toward Alachua, I surprised myself by abruptly leaving the highway, steering between the old hickories Mama had set out and lurching to a stop at the foot of what was left of our former home's front sidewalk. The restaurant had felt nothing like home, but this might be different. Something of us might still be found.

Exhibit A: A ragged paper Camel cigarette package, unexpected because Daddy smoked only Lucky Strikes. Surely those butts I puffed on behind the barn were Luckies. Half the cigarette pack is torn away, but on its back, framed by two Art Deco columns, the R. J. Reynolds Co. informs its customers, "Don't look for premiums or coupons, as the cost of tobacco blended in Camel Cigarettes prohibits the use of them." I don't remember any Camels but, holding this package in my hand, I see vividly my handsome father at forty, a cigarette dangling from between his lips.

Also in this silt-filled Ziploc bag, a wadded-up page from an address book: Mother's handwriting, faded, except for "Alison," whose address was entered three times. A torn piece of newsprint: the Copocabana is suing Sammy Davis, Jr. and the name of Patty Duke's newly born son is Sean. The font looks like that of the *High Springs Herald*; I'm guessing, the 1970s.

Exhibit B: Two rusty nails, one without a head; or is it two pieces of one long nail that fell out when the house was lifted from its concrete footings? Four pieces of wood, quite filthy, one of which must be a shim, I think, because the two-inch width has been shaved at its unweathered end to about a quarter of an inch. A piece of beaded board, also shaved, as though it were used as a wedge between two other timbers. Finally, a two-by-four-inch piece of tongue-and-groove, its paint now reduced to a few thin gray lines.

Exhibit C: Two ancient corncob bits, an olive seashell, and four other whorled shells, small golden tubas perhaps the former homes of garden snails. Eight glued-together bits of white yarn that might be hair from the fabric doll that once hung above my crib. One piece of clear jagged glass; two pine splinters; a wad of tarnished foil (perhaps from Mother's prize Easter egg, hidden beneath the large green leaves of the blue hydrangea); a shard of white tile. The breezeway with jalousies Mother had built had bits of colored tile embedded in its concrete floor. Those jalousies didn't close properly and Mother never traveled the concrete floor from house to car without declaring her dissatisfaction with the jalousie man. Also in this bag, printed instructions and a diagram for self-sticking wallpaper: Mama's green ivy trailing across a white background on her kitchen's pantry wall.

Exhibit D: In its own individual Ziploc bag I find a skeleton, its neck too long for a bird, the toes of its feet curled back. One long-ago evening, the scratchy sounds of a rat's movements inspired me to open the medicine cabinet's door, then stand, galvanized and screaming in the bathroom until Daddy arrived and, plunging an ice pick into the creature, commented, "Shoulda stayed at the barn."

My hands are dirty. From this soil I patted cakes, picked petunias that grew along both sides of the walk, and, as a sweating and reluctant teenager, pulled summer's high weeds. What light does this display cast on our lives? We, like the Native Americans and settlers before us, ate corn and sometimes grew it; Daddy smoked cigarettes; Mama kept an address book and installed wallpaper; bits of newspaper blew under the house; a rat died.

How innocently we lived, my sister and I, playing hide-and-seek, comforting our baby dolls. We suspected nothing of all that has now befallen us, nor that death is only the final one of many difficulties. There is no evidence here of those Christmas mornings when Daddy, hung over, opened his gifts and sobbed, telling us he didn't deserve them; no measure of our griefs nor of an even greater hopefulness that grew as we waited for Christmas.

Do these bits of trash hold our laughter, my punishment when my toddling sister flushed our baby rings while I was assigned to watch her? These wooden shims—if that is what they are—suggest one crucial fact: an attempt was made to get our house level.

I suppose I'd hoped to discover on this desk substantial evidence of the irresistible and overwhelming love my parents and their daughters felt for one another, how greatly we wanted to be happy. That's not here, not unless you can picture a woman in late afternoon light, picking through stones and weeds for trash. The heart's truths bared, even spread out on a desktop, remain unquantifiable.

154

Of my two uncles, Orion and Willie, whose friendship and affection sustained me after my father's death, Uncle Orion is the one I understood best. If Uncle Willie was concerned with making money, Uncle Orion was determined to figure things out; they were the most different of brothers. I stood at my Uncle Willie's deathbed when his pupils were fixed and dilated, but I was in Mississippi the night Orion's wife, Caris, called to say she didn't think he'd last until dawn.

Uncle Orion and I shared the traits that had allowed us once to spend an entire

Uncle Orion's funeral, Antioch Cemetery, 1992. Photograph © Barbara B. Gibbs. Used by permission.

morning together following the movements of a pair of red-winged blackbirds as they built their nest. And we worried certain topics for hours—like why cousin so-and-so came to such a sorry end—usually concluding we'd never know.

Uncle Orion wasn't concerned with progress; in fact, he was highly skeptical of most human enterprise. Once, when I introduced him to a man I was dating and told him I might remarry, he looked soberly at the two of us, shook his head, and said, "Well, Hon-eee, I sure do wish you luck."

Though Uncle Orion told it eloquently, long ago, I have been a long time grasping the truth of human connectedness. In 1976, on the first anniversary of my father's death, distraught and self-pitying after a visit to Daddy's Antioch grave, I stopped at Uncle Orion's house. He, like his son, Leon, laid down words as if they were bricks. The day was cold, and we sat in front of the fireplace. Uncle Orion was wearing a green plaid flannel shirt he said had belonged to Daddy, pants too large for him, and very small shoes. He had a blanket over his lap. "Your daddy's corn sheller," he said, "is out in the barn." My father had got the sheller from his and Orion's father, and now, Uncle Orion said, "Nadine is to have it. One of your daddy's saddles," he added, "is out there, falling apart." He offered to show me the saddle, but I said, "No, I'm not trying to find all of Daddy's stuff at this late date."

Silence. "So," I asked, "is this all there is?"

My uncle leaned forward, picked up an empty tin can from the floor, and lifted it to his mouth. He glanced up, spit a straight stream of tobacco juice, set the can back on the floor, raised his head, and looked straight into me, his brown eyes almost black.

"Hon-eee," he said. "Oh, Hon-eee, you in this with the rest of us."

The epigraph by Jose Ortega y Gasset on page vii comes from Belden Lane's *Landscapes of the Sacred: Geography and Narrative in American Spirituality* (New York/Mahwah: Paulist Press, 1988), p. 16.

PREFACE

1. Carolyn Heilbrun, *Writing a Woman's Life* (New York: Ballantine Books, 1988), p. 15.

2. Will McLean, *Florida Sand: Seminole* (Floral City, FL: The Will McLean Foundation, 1992), p. 17.

CHAPTER 1

1. From my April 1986 interview with my elderly uncles, Orion and Willie Cauthen, captured when I went out of the room and left the tape recorder running.

2. Reproduced from Lawrence A. Clayton, Vernon James Knight, Jr., and Edward E. Moore, eds., *The De Soto Chronicles, Vol. II* (Tuscaloosa: The University of Alabama Press, 1993), endpapers. The insert on the "De Soto Map" in that edition reads as follows:

> This is a modern copy of a pen-and-ink sketch map in the General Archive of the Indies in Seville. The original is unsigned and undated, but it is believed to have been drawn by the Spanish royal cartographer Alonso de Santa Cruz,

among whose papers it was originally found. It is believed to date around 1544 and is the earliest known map giving any detail about the interior of North America. The source of the information was obviously one or more of the survivors of the De Soto expedition. The rendering of the coast comes from other contemporary sources, and the author has attempted, with limited success, to match the coastal river mouths and bays to the rivers crossed in the interior by De Soto's army.

3.   In 1824, the federal government (see *Territorial Papers*) funded work along the Old Spanish Trail that stretched across Florida from St. Augustine to Pensacola, connecting East and West Florida. (Eventually the trail made its way to California.) Admiral Daniel Burch directed the work; for the St. Augustine to Tallahassee portion, he employed John Bellamy. The U.S. Army Corps of Engineers accomplished the leveling and clearing from Tallahassee to Pensacola. Michael Gannon's *New History of Florida* details how the territorial legislature came to meet in 1824 (Florida did not become a state until 1845) at Tallahassee. For a fuller understanding of early Florida roads and trails, see Mark Boyd's article in *Florida Highways* (June 1951) and consult listings under "The Bellamy Road" and "El Camino Real" in Allen Morris's *Florida Place Names* (Sarasota, FL: Pineapple Press, Inc., 1995).

Further, in a 2003 personal note to me, Walt Marder, of the Florida State Bureau of Historic Resources, writes:

> From Pensacola to the Appalachicola River is the "Military Road" Capt. Daniel Burch of the Quartermaster Corps constructed. The length from the Appalachicola to the Ochlocknee River was opened by a second contractor. From there, it was Bellamy's baby to Picolata where it joined the existing road. *The Territorial Papers* mention Joshua

Hickman, William Drummond, Benjamin Chares, and
Francis Ross, as well as John Bellamy, as having worked
portions of the road. The Military Road very occasionally
goes by the name Federal Road. Nowhere does it carry
the moniker Bellamy.

4. The 1966 Antioch "Home Coming" booklet of unknown origin provides
this information about the church my father's family attended when he was a child:

> In the 1880s, this Community had no Churches or
> Schools. There were humble homes dotted here and there,
> a cotton gin known as the Old Scott Gin House, and a fort
> for the protection of the people against Indians during the
> Indian War. The Old Scott Gin House and the fort were
> about three miles south of the present Church building
> on what is now the C. D. Bethea place. These were on the
> Old Bellamy Road, or the main road from St. Augustine
> to Tallahassee . . . . The Old Scott Gin House became the
> first Community meeting place for worship. All the various
> Denominations gathered there, coming by horseback,
> oxcart, horse carts, or walking . . . . The church held foot-
> washing services twice yearly until sometime in the early
> [18]90s. In 1887, work was begun on the second building
> . . . . Old Confederate money, conins [coins], and other
> tokens were dropped in this [corner] stone and sealed. The
> following September this stone was broken and robbed.

5. William Butler Yeats, *The Collected Poems of W. B. Yeats* (New
York: MacMillan Publishing Co., Inc., 1933). Used by permission of
Simon & Schuster, Inc., 1230 Avenue of the Americas, New York, NY
10020.

CHAPTER 2

1. The epigraph comes from my interview with Mary Lou McFadden on July 20, 1987. Vernon (who appears in my text on page 18) was also the name of Vernon McFadden Hill's mother. I published an earlier version of this chapter in *The Orlando Sentinel* (March 26, 1988).

2. The comment comes from her autobiographical book, *Cross Creek* (New York: MacMillan Publishing Company, 1942), p. 3:

> If there be such a thing as racial memory, the consciousness
> of land and water must lie deeper in the core of us than
> any knowledge of our fellow beings. We were bred of earth
> before we were born of our mothers. Once born, we can live
> without mother or father, or any other kin, or any friend or
> any human love. We cannot live without the earth or apart
> from it, and something is shriveled in a man's heart when
> he turns away from it and concerns himself only with the
> affairs of men.

3. This and subsequent quotes within this chapter are from the transcripts of *Alachua Portrait: The Living Heritage Project* (hereafter referred to as AP), a community values clarification project funded by The Florida Humanities Council, 1983-1984, that I directed.

CHAPTER 3

1. From the 1983 AP transcripts.
2. Lucile Skinner Traxler's "The History of Springhill United Methodist Church" (1985) lists foods the men of the church prepared for their Sunday morning breakfast meetings: "Cheese biscuits, fish roe, chicken livers, venison, shark, alligator and quail as well as the traditional ham, eggs, bacon and some

things that would not do to mention." Mrs. Traxler's history was my source for much of the historical detail in this chapter.

3.   The Beatitudes mentioned were spoken by Jesus. They are found in Matthew, Chapter 5, from my Grandfather Strickland's worn *King James Bible*, published by The Saalfield Publishing Co. (Chicago, ca. 1900), p. 1033:

> Blessed are the poor in spirit: for their's [sic] is the kingdom
> of heaven. Blessed are they that mourn: for they shall be
> comforted. Blessed are the meek: for they shall inherit
> the earth. Blessed are they which do hunger and thirst
> after righteousness: for they shall be filled. Blessed are
> the merciful: for they shall obtain mercy. Blessed are
> the pure in heart: for they shall see God. Blessed are the
> peacemakers: for they shall be called the children of God.
> Blessed are they which are persecuted for righteousness'
> sake: for their's [sic] is the kingdom of heaven.

4.   I recorded Letha DeCoursey's story of the mimosa tree in July 1987. With the exception of her statement from the AP transcripts and an interview recorded by Allan Burns for AP in 1983 (see note 5, below), all of DeCoursey's remarks quoted in this essay come from the 1987 interview.

Contrary to Letha's memory of eating the mimosa's pods, I have learned that, at high doses, the pods are considered toxic. Generally speaking, the plant is inedible. The carob (*Ceratonia siliqua*, not *Albizia julibrissin*) is the plant biblical scholars credit with nourishing John the Baptist; but it is conceivable that Letha's mother, in her work as midwife and herbalist, knew of or experimented with *Albizia julibrissin* for medicinal use. The carob is not found in Alachua County.

5.   Allan Burns, of the University of Florida, recorded DeCoursey's report on herbal remedies, such as corn shucks and the uses of cow parts, in a video for AP in 1983.

CHAPTER 4

1. From the 1983 AP transcripts. Steve Everett taught biology at Santa Fe High School. Some of the details in this chapter I published in a notice about the dedication at Bland of a historic marker for Santa Fe de Toloca. The notice appeared in *The Orlando Sentinel* (April 30, 1990). Also, an earlier version of this chapter was previously published in the 1994 Spring/Summer issue of *Crossroads: A Journal of Southern Culture*.

2. Photo credit: The Florida Center for Instructional Technology, University of South Florida, http://fcit.usf.edu/FLORIDA/lessons/lemoyne/lemoyne.htm. On this Website one learns the following:

> Jacques LeMoyne was a French artist who came to Florida with Rene de Laudonniere, a French explorer, in 1564. LeMoyne was the first artist to visit the New World. He traveled through north Florida, charting the coastline and the lives of the Timucua Indians.
>
> When Laudonniere's group arrived, they found that the Indians were worshipping a stone column emblazoned with the French coat of arms. It was located at the mouth of the St. Johns River. Jean Ribault, a French explorer who had been there two years earlier, had set it up as proof of French possession.
>
> Laudonniere and his party sailed about five miles up the St. Johns River. They established a settlement. Then they built Fort Caroline out of wood and sod.
>
> When the Spanish attacked and burned Fort Caroline, LeMoyne and Laudonniere were two of the French who escaped. Almost all of LeMoyne's drawings were burned up. The survivors quickly sailed back to France, where LeMoyne redrew the pictures from memory. Jacques

LeMoyne died in London in 1588.

An engraver named Theodore DeBry made engravings of the drawings that LeMoyne had made of Florida. In 1591, DeBry published a book with the engravings and LeMoyne's description of his trip to Florida. For the first time, Europeans could see what life was like in America without sailing across the Atlantic Ocean.

There is a long-standing argument over the provenance of the work. Some say the engravings we see were supposedly made by DeBry from watercolors that LeMoyne's wife sold after his death. See, for example, Jerald Milanich at http://www.archaeology.org/0505/abstracts/florida.html.

3.   Reproduced from Charlton W. Tebeau, *A History of Florida* (Coral Gables: University of Miami Press, 1971), p. 51. In his book, *The Cross in the Sand: The Early Catholic Church in Florida, 1513–1870* (Gainesville: University Press of Florida, 1992), Michael V. Gannon describes the circumstances surrounding the earliest introduction of Christianity within the United States of America. Beginning with the celebration of the First Mass in St. Augustine, Florida, on September 8, 1565, Gannon details the Franciscan establishment of missions that dotted Florida from St. Augustine to Pensacola, of which Santa Fe de Toloca was considered the principal mission.

Spain's *la Florida* was overseen by the Bishop of Santiago de Cuba, Gabriel Diaz Vara Calderón, whose account of his ten-month visit tells that the "Indians" spent summer nights on the ground, but in winter they slept around fires in crude huts. Their usual diet, Calderón noted, was "corn with ashes, pumpkin, beans," and whatever meat they could find (Gannon, p. 65). The bishop returned to Cuba in late June 1675, where he died a year later, "some say from the hardships endured on his visitation" (p. 66).

4.   Archaeologist Kenneth (Ken) Johnson's research centered on identifying the boundaries between Potano and Utina tribal cultures. Johnson's later work suggests it is possible this woman was not Potano but Utina. I first heard of the

"lost" mission in 1976 from Larry Westmoreland, of High Springs, who had collected artifacts in the area. See Johnson's 1991 University of Florida doctoral dissertation, *The Utina and the Potano Peoples of Northern Florida: Changing Settlement Systems in the Spanish Colonial Period.*

5.   As quoted in Adelaide K. Bullen's *Florida Indians of Past and Present* (Gainesville: Kendall Books, ca. 1950, n.p.). Jerald Milanich, of the University of Florida, suggested the comparison between early exploration of Florida and today's space program.

6.   Mary Lou McFadden spoke of swimming in area sinkholes in her 1987 interview.

7.   See O. B. Hardison, Jr., "The Disappearance of Man" (*The Georgia Review*, Winter 1988, pp. 679-713).

CHAPTER 5

1.   From the 1983 AP transcripts. Arthur Spencer, Jr., is a historian of local and Southern history who retired from teaching history at the Mebane Middle School. Some details in the essay were first published in my story, "A Loving Look at Alachua" (*The Gainesville Sun*, October 18, 1988).

2.   This Greater New Hope Missionary Baptist Church service was recorded by the author on August 7, 1988.

3.   From my interview with Lemon Washington on August 11, 1988.

4.   The anticipated change in tobacco farming and the demise of the small family farm have larger repercussions than whether or not the sons of people such as Malphurs will be able to live as their fathers did, as P. J. Van Blokland points out in "Solving the U. S. Farm Crisis" (Gainesville: Food and Resource Economics Department, Institute of Food and Agricultural Sciences, University of Florida, 1987), p. 4:

>   Family farms contribute something uniquely valuable to
>   a country. This is not a new idea. It was first published by

Cicero and later encouraged by Thomas Jefferson. Despite the move (correctly) towards farming as a business, it will always remain a way of life. We forget this at our peril.

About one in four Americans live in rural areas. As farmers increasingly get into trouble and leave their farms, local services inevitably decline. The farm service businesses follow, leaving lenders in even more trouble. As customers leave, stores close, leaving fewer people more dependent on distant urban centers.

As farm profitability falls, young people that would otherwise farm, look for off-farm opportunities. Local schools, churches and other services close, increasing travel for those remaining. The vacant farms are taken up by larger farmers and, more recently, by farm management companies which now farm some 6% of U.S. row crop land.

Some of this change is necessary. We have always had a fluid society. But rapid changes like this produce depressed rural areas that rival urban depression. At the same time, rural communities are experiencing more 'urban' [sic] sicknesses like crime, alcoholism, drugs, family abuse, and suicides.

Also of note, Charles Reagan Wilson, writing in his and William Ferris's *The Encyclopedia of Southern Culture* (Chapel Hill: University of North Carolina Press, 1989) on "Agribusiness," observes that, by 1970, "Corporations owned one-fifth of Florida's farm acreage" (p. 15).

5. From p. 793 of my Grandfather Strickland's *Bible*.

6. The Spanish Crown awarded grants of land to individuals in the New World, here to J. S. Sanchez, one of a number of parcels of land granted to individuals prior to the Spanish government's ceding of the East and West Floridas to the U.S. in 1821 when Florida became a U.S. Territory. The U.S. Board of

Land Commissioners was established in 1822 to settle all outstanding Spanish land grant claims in the territory. In Alachua County, there is more than one "Sanchez" grant as well as others carrying such names as Atkinson and Arredondo.

7.   In this Baptist church, communion is considered an ordinance or memorial rather than a "sacrament," which Catholics define as an outward sign of an inner grace.

8.   Southern evangelical Protestants would usually call the church ordinance Huldah Malphurs and I discuss "The Lord's Supper," not "Communion." The ordinance is celebrated quarterly in churches such as Huldah's New Oak Grove Baptist Church. For commentary comparing the significance of this version of Communion to those of other religious groups, see Samuel S. Hill, "Introduction to Religion," in Wilson and Ferris, eds., *The Encyclopedia of Southern Culture*, p. 1269.

CHAPTER 6

1.   Personal conversation with Hortense Cauthen, ca. 1983. An earlier version of this chapter was previously published in the Summer 2004 issue of *The Chattahoochee Review*.

2.   Alachua High School became Alachua Elementary in 1956 when Santa Fe High School opened to serve grades 7-12.

CHAPTER 7

1.   From the 1984 AP videotape, "This Place, Alachua," by videographer Ed Wells and me.

2.   Scholars push this date forward and backward, depending on the newest evidence in hand.

3.   For more on this map and others, see Ralph E. Ehrenberg, "*Marvellous countries and lands": Notable Maps of Florida, 1507-1846* at http://www.broward.

org/library/bienes/lii14003.htm. See, also, note 2 from Chapter 4.

4.   Norm LaCoe's remarks about early Newnansville can be found in the AP transcripts.

5.   The easternmost portion of US 441 within the City of Alachua was renamed for Martin Luther King, Jr. immediately prior to a 1984 city election. The road's marker does not include "Jr."

CHAPTER 8

1.   This epigraph and all the other indented quotes in this chapter come from the 1983 AP transcripts, except for the words of the prayer that bring this chapter to a close. The prayer is copied from the *Alachua Women's Club Program* (1991).

2.   Grandfather of Southern religious studies, Samuel S. Hill, Jr., says in "Introduction to Religion," from Wilson and Ferris's *The Encyclopedia of Southern Culture*, p. 1274, "The American South perpetuates a distinctive type of religion. Although different only in degree from forms of Christianity found elsewhere, the degree is decisive. The *standard* form in the South is normative for all forms, and the linkage between faith and the regional culture is intimate." Hill describes Granddaddy Strickland's Baptists, along with Methodists, as the "big two; . . . the Southern way of life is a Protestant way of life." In its homogeneity, the South is unique. Hill declares, "in every other American region, a genuine pluralism [of religious views] prevails."

3.   In regard to the marriage of religion and pro-slavery positions, Charles Reagan Wilson, in *Baptized in Blood* (Athens: University of Georgia Press, 1989), says, "For a generation, they had preached slavery's divine nature and the need to protect it" (p. 14).

4.   The creation of Mebane Middle School in Alachua soon after the 1954 Supreme Court decision, *Brown v. Board of Education*, demonstrates what Charles Reagan Wilson, in his and William Ferris's *The Encyclopedia of Southern Culture*, p. 586, calls the response of a "siege mentality." By this I understand Wilson to mean the complex experience of Southern history that includes a decided defensiveness

regarding racial matters. For a fuller discussion, see Charles Reagan Wilson's "Introduction to History and Manners" in *The Encyclopedia of Southern Culture.*

5.   Foevrin is not to be confused with Ralph Cellon, Jr., or any other actual person. I have attributed to the fictitious Foevrin many actions by several people whom I personally witnessed or was told about in confidence by credible informants. These descriptions of Foevrin belong to no one person but to many of the city's political figures since 1905. Although I made Foevrin male, to my knowledge—at the time this chapter was written—there had also been three female commissioners.

6.   This confrontation took place between me and a person whose name I prefer not to reveal.

7.   See the photo of Mr. Sealey's store on page 87.

CHAPTER 9

1.   From my May 1988 interview with Nancy Meggs McWhinnie.

2.   Rosemary Bryant's house sat opposite Mother's in Alachua, and they were friends. In late summer 1991, Rosemary went to Orlando to assist with Mother's care.

3.   My understanding of Southern individualism and Victorianism was influenced by Wilbur J. Cash's *The Mind of the South* (New York: Random House, 1941) and Daniel Joseph Singal's *The War Within: From Victorian to Modernist Thought, 1919-1945* (University of North Carolina, 1982).

4.   Joe Akerman, in his book, *Florida Cowman: A History of Florida Cattle Raising* (Kissimmee, FL: Florida Cattleman's Association, 1977), discusses the significance of Florida's beef for the Confederate Army.

5.   The details of the woven baby carriage are in Hortense Meggs Cauthen's 1985 interview, conducted by Mary Elizabeth Irby.

6.   This chapter takes its title from the song recorded by Mark Chesnutt on the album, *Too Cold at Home* (Universal City: MCA Records, Inc. 1990). It is used by permission of Hal Leonard, Corp., 7777 West Bluemound Road, Post Office

Box 13819, Milwaukee, Wisconsin 53213.

7.   I called my parents' first child, Allen Cauthen, Jr. (who died the day he was born: December 26, 1941), "little brother." I was born January 13, 1943.

8.   The folk account of the Millhopper's beginnings was collected by the WPA Writers of Florida, but I remember best "Cousin Thelma" Boltin's version rendered many times for the Alachua County Folk Arts Program.

9.   Henry Wadsworth Longfellow, *The Song of Hiawatha* (Boston: Ticknor and Fields, 1856), p. 39.

10.   Hortense Cauthen's story of children playing in coffee weeds was copied in longhand during October 1991; I took the tape recorder to Orlando, but I never had the heart to turn it on. Hortense Cauthen's other memories are from my interview on February 13, 1985.

11.   See the LeMoyne/DeBry plate on page 33.

12.   In *Trabelin' On: The Slave Journey to an Afro-Baptist Faith* (Princeton: Princeton University Press, 1988), p. 115, Mechal Sobel's intriguing study of how African beliefs melded with the Christianity of slaves, she presents these startling statements:

> In Africa, white was symbolic of goodness, purity,
> and holiness, while black symbolized evil. This color
> consciousness and value judgment runs throughout
> the West African world view . . . . Black as evil has deep
> roots, perhaps universal in nature, and is no doubt tied
> to fear of night and darkness and loss of the sun...

CHAPTER 10

1.   From the 1983 AP transcripts. This chapter is drawn from personal observation, conversations with Alachuans, and newspaper accounts from *The High Springs Herald, Gainesville Sun, Alachua Today,* and *Alachua Observer.*

2.   Leon's property is located within Alachua County's Section 18, Township

8, Range 20. A section of land is 640 acres or one square mile.

3.   Most notably, these books include: *The Others: How the Animals Made Us Human* (Island Press/Shearwater Books, 1995) and *Man in the Landscape: An Historic View of the Esthetics of Nature* (New York: Alfred A. Knopf, 1967), by Paul Shephard; *The Ecocriticism Reader: Landmarks in Literature Ecology,* edited by Cheryll Glotfelty and Harold Fromm (Athens: University of Georgia Press, 1996); *The Green Breast of the New World: Landscape, Gender, and American Fiction,* by Louise H. Westling (Athens: University of Georgia Press, 1996); *The Environmental Imagination: Thoreau, Nature Writing, and the Formation of American Culture,* by Lawrence Buell (Cambridge, MA: The Belknap Press, 1995); *The Spell of the Sensuous: Perception and Language in a More-Than-Human World,* by David Abram (New York: Vintage Books, 1997); and *The Idea of Wilderness: From Prehistory to the Age of Egology,* by Max Oelschlaeger (New Haven: Yale University Press, 1995).

4.   See James Howard Kunstler, *The Geography of Nowhere: The Rise and Decline of American's Man-made Landscape* (New York: Simon & Schuster, 1993).

5.   I first took note of this in *Audubon* Magazine (July–August, 2001). See, also, Al Gore, *An Inconvenient Truth: The Planetary Emergency of Global Warming and What We Can Do About It* (Emmaus, PA: Rodall Publishing, 2006).

6.   From the 1983 AP transcripts.

7.   As quoted in Mark Van Doren, ed., *The Travels of William Bartram* (New York: Dover Publications, 1955) p. 90.

8.   As quoted in Mark Van Doren, p. 173.

9.   In 1999, Florida set a national precedent by winning a $13.1 billion lawsuit (and settling for $11.3 billion) against tobacco companies. Afterward, the governor's cabinet lifted its ban on Florida's investing in tobacco shares. A cabinet member, reported the *St. Pete Times,* commented, "What's important is maximum return, not social and political statements."

10. From my telephone conversation with Clovis Watson on April 1, 2006.

11. As quoted in Mark Van Doren, p. 173 (see note 7, above).

g l o s s a r y
o f f l o r i d a
p l a c e s

The following information about places mentioned frequently in the text is based, first and foremost, on Allen Morris's *Florida Place Names* (Sarasota, FL: Pineapple Press, Inc.; 1995) as well as *Alachua County: A Sesquicentennial Tribute* (Alachua County Historical Commission, 1976); *Antioch Church Homecoming Booklet* (1966); B. E. Bloodworth's *Florida Place-Names* (Gainesville: University of Florida Press, 1959); *Merriam-Webster's Geographical Dictionary, Third* Edition (Springfield, MA: Merriam-Webster, 1997); Alfred G. Bradbury's *A Chronology of Florida Post Offices* (Florida Federation of Stamp Clubs, 1962); F. W. Buchholz's *History of Alachua County* (St. Augustine, FL: The Record Company, 1929); Jess G. Davis's *History of Alachua County, Florida* (Gainesville: Alachua County Historical Commission, 1959); Charlotte M. Porter's *William Bartram's Florida: A Naturalist's Vision. The Teacher's Manual* (Gainesville: Florida Museum of Natural History, ca. 1989), p. 17; and William A. Read's *Florida Place Names of Indian Origin and Seminole Personal Names* (Baton Rouge: Louisiana State University Press, 1934). Population figures are from the 2000 U.S. Census.

Alachua, the city:
Population, 6,098; post office established in 1887; town incorporated in 1905. Alachua is an Indian name associated since the early eighteenth century with several area locations, including Payne's Prairie State Preserve (William Bartram's Alachua Savanna); the modern town of Alachua; the county, of which Gainesville is the county seat; and a Creek Indian settlement spelled "Allachua," which appears on 1715, 1720, and 1733 maps.

Alachua, the county:

Population, 220,054; Gainesville is the county seat. When the county was given this name in 1824, its original boundaries stretched from the Georgia-Florida line to Port Charlotte Harbor, 100 miles south of present-day Tampa. "La Chua" was the name of the Spaniards' largest cattle ranch.

Natives usually explain "Alachua" as an Indian name meaning "big jug without a bottom." At one time the name also designated a large lake two and one-half miles south of Gainesville traveled by river boats during the nineteenth century until, unexpectedly, the lake drained. The flat marshy area that remains is called "Payne's Prairie" after Seminole Chieftain, King Payne, who led the Seminoles from Georgia into Florida in 1750. Payne was killed in a battle led by Col. Dan Newnan during the 1812 territorial war.

Antioch Baptist Church and Cemetery:

The nineteenth-century Antioch Baptist Church and its cemetery, located halfway between the city of LaCrosse and the settlement of Monteocha, grew out of an interdenominational meeting place which, until 1887, met at the Old Scott Gin House where foot washing services were held twice yearly. In 1887, work was begun on the second [actually the third location, if we count the "bush arbor"] church building. Confederate money placed in its cornerstone was stolen a few months later.

Bat Cave:

South of Alachua, the cave is five miles northwest of the town of Newberry at the western edge of Alachua County where live oak and wild cherry are plentiful, although the surrounding acreage is used for the growing of slash pine. The water table pools in the lowest portions of the cave where crayfish, crickets, and fossilized remains of the white-tailed deer (*Odocoileus virginianus*) have been found. The cave has recently been deeded to Santa Fe Community College in Gainesville, which uses it as an educational site.

Bellamy Road, The:

In 1824, the U.S. Congress authorized and funded the opening and clearing of "The Old Spanish Road" between St. Augustine and Pensacola in what was then Territorial Florida. John Bellamy, of St. Augustine, was paid $13,500 for his work on the road's eastern route, which, in order to avoid spots sometimes underwater, deviated from the original. Local inhabitants attached his name to the road.

Bland:

In 1903, a rural post office opened seven miles north of Alachua and Postmaster J. L. Matthews gave it the name of his eldest son. The post office closed in 1906.

Cross Creek:

This area, settled in the 1880s, was made famous by Marjorie Kinnan Rawlings in her novel, *The Yearling* (1938), which won a Pulitzer Prize. Parts of the movie *Cross Creek,* based on Rawling's 1942 autobiographical book describing her discovery of her Florida home, were filmed in nearby Evinston and in Micanopy.

Florida:

Population, 15,982,378 (fourth in the U.S.); granted statehood in 1845. This first place on the North American continent named by Europeans stretched all the way to the Mississippi River when Spain (in exchange for Cuba) ceded it to Britain in 1763. When Juan Ponce de Leon first caught sight of the Florida mainland on Easter Sunday in 1513, he claimed it for the Spanish Crown and called it *Pasqua de Flores.* Modern Florida is now home to more than 150 ethnic groups.

Gainesville:

Population, 95,447. The area was known as Potano Province when Hernando de Soto came through in 1539. Gainesville, created in 1854 as the county seat for Alachua County, was incorporated as a city in 1869. It was named for Gen. Edmund Pendleton Gaines, known for his capture of Aaron Burr and for commanding U.S. Army troops during the Second Seminole War. At the time of Florida's secession from the Union in 1861, nearly half the town's white inhabitants were Florida-born, and half of those were of South Carolinian descent. The University of Florida (founded in 1853) and Santa Fe Community College (1966) are located here.

Hague:
Post office established in 1883; closed in 1929. This community once had a grist mill, cotton gin, two sawmills, a school, and it was a railway stop from which local crops were shipped to market.

High Springs:
Population, 3,863; incorporated in 1892. High Springs was first called Santaffey (which had a post office in 1884), then Orion (and a second post office, in 1886), before it got a name that stuck in 1888. In the early twentieth century, the town sprung up around its rail yard and railway maintenance shops, and it also became an agricultural and mining center. It is seven miles northwest of Alachua on US 441, and its historic architecture and antique stores attract many tourists.

LaCrosse:
Post office established in 1881; incorporated in 1897. A state historical marker gives credit for its name to settlers from LaCrosse, Wisconsin. The town sits midway between Santa Fe and Monteocha, north of Gainesville. At the turn of the twentieth century, it had several stores, board sidewalks, a cotton gin, and a hotel. Cotton, then potatoes, were its chief exports. The LaCrosse Potato Growers' brick building still stands.

Lafayette County:
Population, 7,022; established in 1856. Located northwest of Alachua County, Lafayette is Florida's thirty-third county, named in honor of the Marquis de Lafayette, supporter of the American Revolution and friend of Richard Keith Call, an early Florida governor.

Monteocha:
Historically, Monteocha is a farming community near the portion of the Bellamy Road that passes through east Alachua County. The name was first applied to an African-American settlement.

Newberry:
Population, 3,316; post office established in 1894. Located in the southwestern part of Alachua County, Newberry was developed following the arrival of the Savannah, Florida and Western Railroad. By 1896, Newberry had fourteen phosphate mines, employing 500 men.

Newnansville Cemetery and Old Newnansville:
Dell's Post Office, established here in 1826, was renamed Newnansville in 1837, closed in 1874, then reopened in 1875. Finally, in 1895, mail was redirected to Alachua. Only a cemetery now marks this spot one and one-half miles northeast of Alachua. The location of one of Florida's earliest inland communities, its fort was a sanctuary for settlers during the Indian Wars of the early nineteenth century. Florida's first Methodist Church was established here. In 1828, Newnansville became Alachua County's county seat; the federal land grant office was here. In 1854, voters moved official functions to the newly created county seat, Gainesville. Because all but its cemetery has disappeared, some folks refer to Newnansville as "Old Newnansville"; they are the same place.

Nokomis:
Population, 3,334; in Sarasota County. In Henry Wadsworth Longfellow's *Hiawatha (1856)*, Nokomis is the mother of Wenonah, which, in Ojibway, means "my grandmother." In Menomini legend, this is the name of the grandmother of all humankind and of Manabush, the Menomini hero-god. Nokomis lies south of the City of Sarasota.

Olustee:

The small town of Olustee in Baker County had a post office from 1830 to 1930, but it is now a ghost town. Florida's major Civil War conflict, the Battle of Olustee, was fought here and is reenacted annually. In this battle, Union losses were so dramatic that federal forces afterwards spoke of the fight as the second Dade Massacre. This location is also known as Ocean Pond.

Payne's Prairie:

Known earlier as the Alachua Savannah, Payne's Prairie, an open plain of 20,000 acres, is now a state preserve. Over many centuries, its character has changed: today it is comprised of grasses and marsh; when William Bartram arrived in 1774 it was dry, but, during the late nineteenth century, ferry boats traveled across its waters. In recent years, bison have been brought back to the prairie from which they had long ago disappeared.

Providence:

Post office established August 4, 1864; closed on March 29, 1867; reopened September 22, 1874; closed for the second time on September 15, 1906. In her *Gainesville Sun* column "Yesterday," on June 30, 1991, Barbara Crawford reported that the hamlet was a prosperous place in antebellum days; in 1885, Providence was shipping oats, corn, cotton, potatoes, peas, beans, and oranges. This agricultural community, which dates from 1830 and was once as busy as Traxler, is now little more than a Union County crossroads with a family-owned feed store.

San Felasco Hammock Preserve State Park:

The southeastern section of this 6,500-acre state preserve was the site of the seventeenth-century Spanish mission, San Francisco de Potano. The terrain varies: swamps, hardwood hammocks, pine forests, and sandhills. It is now a part of the Florida State Parks System, which identifies the source of the preserve's name as the "mispronunciation by settlers, and Indians" of the name of the Spanish mission.

Santa Fe and Santa Fe River:
Post office established in 1900; changed to "Rural Station, Alachua" in 1960. The modern town of Santa Fe took its Spanish name from the nearby river, as did the Franciscan mission of Santa Fe de Toloca. "Santa Fe," however, is not the first name given this river that divides Alachua and Columbia counties. *Narratives of the Career of Hernando de Soto*, edited by Edward Gaylor Bourne (New York: Allerton Book Co., 1922), includes the *Diary of Rodrigo Ranjel*, who reported that the river was first named Discords.

The Santa Fe River flows from eastern Alachua County west-southwest into the Suwannee River, which empties into the Gulf of Mexico at Suwannee. The Santa Fe is approximately seventy miles in length.

Tallahassee:
Population 150,624; incorporated in 1825. Said to mean "old town"; as a settlement for aborigines, the state's capital dates back to 1539 when Hernando de Soto met here with the Apalachee. The Spanish mission of San Luis was established here in 1633. The town was chosen as the capital of Florida in 1824 when Florida was still a territory, and it began to be inhabited by settlers only as recently as 1825-1826. The Florida State University (founded in 1851), Florida A & M University (1887), and Tallahassee Community College (1965) are located here.

Traxler:
Post office established in 1891; closed in 1906. Located near the intersection of I-75 and the Bellamy Road, this was once the site of a commissary, cotton gin, grist mill, and post office which served many farm families. This community is now residential.

Waters Pond:
Located in Gilchrist County (which was split off from Alachua County in 1925) and composed of a public park with a boat ramp and a few small fishing cabins in

1975 when the author lived there, this area thirty miles west of Gainesville is now encircled by subdivisions. According to local legend, Waters Pond was visited by the naturalist William Bartram during his 1774 Florida travels. He would have passed near here on his way west toward present-day Oldtown on the Suwannee River.

Abram, David. *The Spell of the Sensuous: Perception and Language in a More-Than-Human World* (New York: Vintage Books, 1997).

Akerman, Joe. *Florida Cowman: A History of Florida Cattle Raising* (Kissimmee, FL: Florida Cattleman's Association, 1976).

Alachua City Directory (Alachua: 1932–1933).

Alachua County: A Sesquicentennial Tribute (Gainesville: The Alachua County Historical Commission, 1974).

Alachua Planning and Zoning Manual, 1986 (Alachua: 1986).

Alachua Portrait: The Living Heritage Project (Alachua: 1983–1984).

Alachua Women's Club Program, 1991 (Alachua: 1991).

Antioch Cemetery Records.

Bailey, Kenneth K. "Protestantism and Afro-Americans in the Old South: Another Look," in *The Journal of Southern History* (November 1975): 451–72.

Baker, Judi, and Tim Check. *City of Alachua Needs Assessment Survey* (Alachua: City of Alachua, 1982).

Banks, Ann. *First-Person America* (New York: Alfred A. Knopf, 1980).

Banks, Roger. *Living in a Wild Garden* (New York: St. Martin's Press, 1982.

Bell, C. Ritchie. "Kudzu," in Charles Reagan Wilson and William Ferris, eds., *The Encyclopedia of Southern Culture* (Chapel Hill: University of North Carolina Press, 1989), p. 383.

Bell, C. Ritchie and Bryan Taylor. *Florida Wildflowers and Roadside Plants* (Chapel Hill: Laurel Hill Press, 1982).

Berry, Wendell. *Recollected Essays, 1965–1980* (San Francisco: North Point Press, 1968).

Bloodworth, Bertha Ernestine. "Florida Place-Names," Ph.D. diss., University of Florida, 1959.

Blumenson, John. *Identifying American Architecture* (New York: W. W. Norton & Company, 1981).

Boltin, Thelma. Oral performance, "The Legend of the Devil's Millhopper," Morningside Nature Center, Gainesville, FL, 1976.

Boyd, Mark F. "The First American Road in Florida: Pensacola-St. Augustine Highway, 1824," in *Florida Historical Quarterly*, Vol. 14, Nos. 2 and 3 (1935): 72 and 192.

Buchholtz, F. W. *History of Alachua County* (St. Augustine, FL.: The Record Company, 1929).

Buell, Lawrence. *The Environmental Imagination: Thoreau, Nature Writing, and the Formation of American Culture* (Cambridge, MA: The Belknap Press, 1995).

Bullen, Adelaide K. *Florida Indians of Past and Present* (Gainesville: Kendall Books, ca.1950).

Bush, David. Interviews with Vada Horner, Alachua, FL: January 20, February 1, and July 1, 1991.

Canot, Captain Theodore. *Adventures of an African Slaver* (New York: Dover Publications, 1969).

Cash, Wilbur J. *The Mind of the South* (New York: Random House, 1941).

Caudle, Everett. "Settlement Patterns in Alachua County, Florida, 1850–1860," in *Florida Historical Quarterly*, Vol. 73 (Spring 1989): 428–40.

Cauthen, Allen. Interview with the author, Alachua, FL: April 10, 1973.

Cauthen, Hortense Meggs. Interviews with the author, Alachua and Orlando, FL: February 13, 1985 and September 11, 1991.

———. Interview with Mary Elizabeth Irby, Alachua, FL: January 30, 1985.

Cauthen, Orion. Interviews with the author, Monteocha and Gainesville, FL: June

4, 1977, November 19, 1984, and January 10 and 16, 1985.

Cauthen, Orion, and Willie Cauthen. Interviews with the author, Gainesville, FL: April 14 and 17, 1986.

Cauthen, Sudye. "Alachua, Florida: A Study of One Southern Place," Master's thesis, University of Mississippi, 1993.

Cauthen, Sudye, and Ed Wells. "This Place, Alachua," a videotape produced at the University of Florida School of Journalism and Communications, 1984.

Cauthen, Willie Earl. Interview with the author, Alachua, FL: February 5, 1984.

Cellon, Frank. Personal conversations with the author, Gainesville, FL: 1983–1990.

Cellon, Ralph W., Sr. Interviews with the author, Hague, FL: June 6 and 14, 1987.

Chesnutt, Mark. *Too Cold at Home* (Universal City: MCA Records, Inc., 1990).

Dampier, Chester Ollie. Interviews with the author, Alachua, FL: December 10, 1986, and October 20, 1987.

Daniel, Pete. *Standing at the Crossroads* (New York: Hill and Wang, 1986).

Davis, Jess G. *History of Alachua County, Florida* (Gainesville: Alachua County Historical Commission, 1959).

DeCoursey, Letha Wright. Videotaped interview with Allan Burns, Alachua, FL: from *Alachua Portrait: The Living Heritage Project*, funded by the Florida Endowment for the Humanities, 1983.

_____. Interviews with the author, Alachua, FL: *From the Bellamy Road: Alachua's Beginnings*, a project funded by Talquin/Florida Progress, August 1, 1987, and August 10, 1988.

DeCoursey, Walter. Personal conversation with the author, Alachua, FL: July 4, 1988.

Doke, Lacy Lancaster. Interviews with the author, Santa Fe, FL: February 13, 1988, and February 11 and 12, 1989, in *From the Bellamy Road: Alachua's Beginnings*, a project funded by Talquin/Florida Progress.

Dollard, John. *Caste and Class in a Southern Town* (New Haven: Yale University Press, 1937).

Duke, George, Sr. Personal conversation with the author, Alachua, FL: April 5, 1983.

Eighmy, John Lee. *Churches in Cultural Captivity* (Knoxville: University of Tennessee Press, 1972).

Ellerbe, Helen, ed. *Alachua County Historical Tour Series* (Gainesville, FL: Alachua County Historical Commission, 1986).

Ellis, Lucile. Interview with the author, Alachua, FL: September 10, 1976.

Enneis, Bill, Sr. Personal correspondence with the author, Alachua, FL: April 1, 1991.

Evans, Gerry. Personal conversations with the author, Alachua, FL: 1976-1979.

Fairbanks, Charles, and Gerald Milanich. *Florida Archaeology* (New York: Academic Press, Inc., 1980).

Foster, Gaines M. "Woodward and Southern Identity", in *The Southern Review*, Vol. 21, No. 2 (Spring 1985): 351–60.

Frazier, Marvin. Interview with the author, Alachua, FL: September 19, 1988.

The Gainesville Sun, Gainesville, FL: "A Loving Look at Alachua" (October 16, 1988).

Gannon, Michael V. *The Cross in the Sand: The Early Catholic Church in Florida, 1513–1870, 2nd Edition* (Gainesville: University Press of Florida, 1992).

_____. *Florida: A Short History* (Gainesville: University Press of Florida, 1993).

_____, ed. *The New History of Florida* (Gainesville: University Press of Florida, 1996).

Gay, James. Interview with the author, LaCrosse, FL: January 20, 1991.

Glotfelty, Cheryll, and Harold Fromm, eds. *The Ecocriticism Reader: Landmarks in Literature Ecology.* (Athens: University of Georgia Press, 1996).

Greater New Hope Missionary Baptist Church service, recorded by the author, Bland, FL: August 7, 1988.

Hardison, O. B., Jr. "The Disappearance of Man," in *The Georgia Review* (Winter 1989): 679–713.

Harrar, Ellwood, and George Harrar. *Guide to Southern Trees* (New York: Dover Publications, Inc., 1946, 1962).

Haworth, Esther Bernice. *Jottings and Echoes Related to Newnansville, One of Florida's Earliest Settlements of Alachua and Columbia Counties* (Gainesville, FL: Shorter Printing Company, Inc., 1975).

Heilbrun, Carolyn G. *Writing a Woman's Life* (New York: W. W. Norton & Co., 1988).

High Springs Herald, High Springs, FL: Features by Sue Allen (Sudye) Cauthen, 1960–1962; features and coverage of Alachua City Commission Meeting by Sudye Cauthen, 1987–1988.

Hildreth, Charles, and Merlin Cox. *History of Gainesville, Florida, 1854-1979* (Gainesville: Alachua County Historical Commission, 1981).

Hill, Samuel S., Jr. "Introduction to Religion," in Charles Reagan Wilson and William Ferris, eds., *The Encyclopedia of Southern Culture*. (Chapel Hill University of North Carolina Press, 1989), pp. 1269–75.

_____. *Religion and the Solid South* (Nashville: Abingdon Press, 1972).

_____. *Southern Churches in Crisis* (New York: Holt, Rinehart and Winston, 1966).

Hill, Vernon McFadden. Interview with the author, Traxler, FL: July 7, 1987.

Historic Alachua: The Good Life Community (Alachua: Alachua Chamber of Commerce, 1989).

Holy Bible, Containing the Old and New Testaments: Translated out of the Original Tongues and with the Former Translations Diligently Compared and Revised, by his Majesty's Special Command (Akron, OH: The Saalfield Publishing Co., ca. 1900).

Hudson, Charles. *The Southeastern Indians* (Knoxville: University of Tennessee Press, 1976).

Isaac, Rhys. *The Transformation of Virginia, 1740–1790* (Chapel Hill: University of North Carolina Press, in association with the Institute of Early American History and Culture, 1982).

Jahoda, Gloria. *The Other Florida* (New York: Charles Scribner's Sons, 1967).

Johnson, Kenneth W. "The Utina and the Potano Peoples of Northern Florida Changing Settlement Systems in the Spanish Colonial Period." Ph.D. diss University of Florida, 1991.

_____. Interview with the author at the archaeological site, Santa Fe de Toloca, Bland, FL: March 17, 1989.

Jones, Peter, ed. *The Making of a Continent* (British Broadcasting Corporation Television, in association with WTTW/Chicago, 1983).

Judd, Danielle. (Alachua Assistant City Manager). Telephone conversation with the author, March 25, 2007.

Kunstler, James Howard. *The Geography of Nowhere: The Rise and Decline of America's Man-made Landscape* (New York: Simon and Schuster, 1994).

Lane, Belden. *Landscapes of the Sacred* (Mahwah, NJ: Paulist Press, 1988).

Lane, Frederic, Eric Goldman, and Erling Hunt, eds. *The World's History* (New York: Harcourt, Brace and Company, 1984).

Lawson, Charles. Interview with the author, Alachua, FL: August 25, 1988, from *Alachua Portrait: The Living Heritage Project*, funded by the Florida Endowment for the Humanities.

Levine, Lawrence W. *Black Culture and Black Consciousness* (Oxford: Oxford University Press, 1977).

Longfellow, Henry Wadsworth. *Hiawatha* (New York: Dial Books for Young Readers, Penguin Press, 1983; originally published in 1856).

Longstreth, Richard. *The Buildings of Main Street* (Washington, DC: The Preservation Press, 1987).

Lundy, Alexander. Interview with the author, Alachua, FL: September 14, 1988.

Lytle, Andrew. "Afterword: A Semicentennial," in the collection *Why the South Will Survive* (Athens: University of Georgia Press, 1981), pp. 224-29.

Malphurs, Huldah Rivers. Interviews with the author, Bland, FL: February 3 and August 14, 1988.

Malphurs, Thomas. Interview with the author, Mayo, FL: October 23, 1987.

Marder, Walt. Personal correspondence with the author, 2003–2006.

Martin, Laura. *Wildflower Folklore* (Charlotte, NC: East Winds Press, 1984).

McFadden, Mary Lou. Interview with the author, Traxler, FL, July 1, 1987, in *From the Bellamy Road: Alachua's Beginnings*, a project funded by Talquin Florida Progress.

McWhinnie, Nancy Meggs. Interview with the author, Mt. Dora, FL: May 17, 1988.

Milanich, Jerald T. Public presentation at the "Spanish Pathways" Conference (Tampa: Florida Endowment for the Humanities, December 1988).

Milanich, Jerald T., and Charles H. Fairbanks. *Florida Archaeology* (New York Academic Press, Inc., 1980).

Morris, Allen. *Florida Place Names* (Sarasota: Pineapple Press, Inc., 1995).

Moses, Galen. "Tobacco Keeps 'Em Farming," in *The Gainesville Sun* (April 18, 1984).

Neeley, Fullward. Personal conversation with the author, Alachua, FL: July 4, 1987.

Nelson, Gil. *Florida's Best Native Landscape Plants: 200 Readily Available Species for Homeowners and Professionals* (Gainesville: University Press of Florida, 2003).

Niering, William A., and Nancy C. Olmstead. *The Audubon Society Field Guide to North American Wildflowers* (New York: Alfred A. Knopf, 1979).

Oelschlaeger, Max. *The Idea of Wilderness: From Prehistory to the Age of Ecology* (New Haven: Yale University Press, 1993).

The Old Farmer's 1987 Almanac (Dublin, NH: Yankee Publishing, 1986).

Opdyke, John, ed. *Alachua County: A Sesquicentennial Tribute* (Gainesville: Alachua County Historical Commission, 1974).

Ownby, Ted. *Subduing Satan: Religion, Recreation, and Manhood in the Rural South, 1865–1920* (Chapel Hill: University of North Carolina Press, 1990).

Poppeliers, John C., Allen Chambers, Jr., and Nancy B. Schwartz. *What Style Is It?* (Washington, DC: The Preservation Press, 1983).

Porter, Charlotte M. *William Bartram's Florida: A Naturalist's Vision. The Teacher's Manual* (Gainesville: Florida Museum of Natural History, ca. 1989).

Preston, Howard L. "Roads and Trails," in Charles Reagan Wilson and Wiliam Ferris, eds., *The Encyclopedia of Southern Culture* (Chapel Hill: University of North Carolina Press, 1989), pps. 1451–52.

Rawlings, Marjorie. *Cross Creek* (New York: MacMillan Publishing Company, 1942).

Read, William A. *Florida Place Names of Indian Origin and Seminole Personal Names* (Baton Rouge: Louisiana State University Press, 1934).

Reed, John Shelton. "The Sociology of Regional Groups," in Lytle, Andrew, *One South: An Ethnic Approach to Regional Culture* (Baton Rouge: Louisiana State University Press, 1982).

Richardson, Mattie. Interview with the author, Alachua, FL: September 13, 1988, in *From the Bellamy Road: Alachua's Beginnings*, a project funded by Talquin/Florida Progress.

Robarts, W. T. "The Fifth Revision to a Historical Sketch of Methodism" (Alachua, FL: The First Methodist Church of Alachua, ca. 1939).

Shepard, Paul. *The Others: How the Animals Made Us Human* (Washington, DC Island Press/Shearwater Books, 1995).

_____. *Man in the Landscape: An Historic View of the Esthetics of Nature* (New York: Alfred A. Knopf, 1967).

Sobel, Mechal. *Trabelin' On: The Slave Journey to an Afro-Baptist Faith* (Princeton Princeton University Press, 1988).

Sosna, Morton. *In Search of the Silent South* (New York: Columbia University Press, 1977).

Spencer, Arthur P. "The World Wars," in *Alachua County: A Sesquicentennial Tribute* (Gainesville: The Alachua County Historical Commission, 1974).

Spencer, Arthur Jr. Interview with the author, Alachua, FL: July 1, 1983.

———. Personal conversations with the author, Alachua, FL: 1975–2007.

Stott, William. *Documentary Expression and Thirties America* (Chicago: University of Chicago Press, 1986).

Tebeau, Charlton W. *A History of Florida* (Coral Gables: University of Miami Press, 1971).

Terkel, Studs. *Hard Times: An Oral History of the Great Depression* (New York Pantheon, 1970), p. 17.

The Territorial Papers, Vols. 22-26, Territory of Florida, 1824–1845.

Traxler, Lucile Skinner. "The History of Springhill United Methodist Church" (Traxler, FL, 1985).

———. Interview with the author, Traxler, FL: February 9, 1988.

Tyree, Allen B. Personal conversations with the author, Jasper, FL: August 15, 2003, and March 1, 2006.

Van Blokland, P. J. "Solving the U.S. Farm Crisis, Staff Paper 304" (Gainesville: Institute of Food and Agricultural Sciences, 1987).

Van Doren, Mark, ed. *Travels of William Bartram* (New York: Dover Publications, 1955).

Vaughn, Cheryl. Personal conversation with the author, High Springs, FL: August 1987.

Vaughn, Millard. Personal conversations with the author, High Springs, FL: 1987–2007.

Walker, Alice. *In Search of Our Mothers' Gardens* (New York: Harcourt, Brace, Jovanovich, 1983).

Washington, Lemon. Interview with the author, Bland, FL: August 11, 1988, in *From the Bellamy Road: Alachua's Beginnings*, a project funded by Talquin/Florida Progress.

Watson, Clovis. Telephone interview with the author, April 1, 2006.

Watts, May Theilgaard. *Reading the Landscape in America* (New York: MacMillan, 1957).

Webber, Carl. *The Eden of the South, Descriptive of the Orange Groves, Vegetable Farms, Strawberry Fields, Peach Orchards, Soil, Climate, Natural Peculiarities, and the People of Alachua County, Florida* (New York: Leve and Alden's Publication Department, 1883).

Welch, Fiermon. Personal conversations with the author, Alachua, FL: 1983–1990.

Westling, Louise H. *The Green Breast of the New World: Landscape, Gender, and American Fiction* (Athens: University of Georgia Press, 1996).

Williams, Emery. Videotaped interview with the author, Alachua, FL: August 20, 1984, from *Alachua Portrait: The Living Heritage Project*, funded by the Florida Endowment for the Humanities.

Williams, Emery. Interview with Evelyn Holland, Alachua, FL: June 27, 1984, from the *Alachua Portrait: The Living Heritage Project*, funded by the Florida Endowment for the Humanities.

Wilson, Charles Reagan. *Baptized in Blood* (Athens: University of Georgia Press, 1989).

————. "Crackers," in Wilson, Charles Reagan, and William Ferris, eds., *The Encyclopedia of Southern Culture* (Chapel Hill: University of North Carolina Press, 1989), p. 1132.

————. "Introduction to History and Manners," in Wilson, Charles Reagan, and William Ferris, eds., *The Encyclopedia of Southern Culture* (Chapel Hill: University of North Carolina Press, 1989), pp. 583-99.

————. ed., *Religion in the South* (Jackson: University Press of Mississippi, 1985).

Wilson, Charles Reagan, and William Ferris, eds. *The Encyclopedia of Southern Culture* (Chapel Hill: University of North Carolina Press, 1989).

Wise, Gene. *American Historical Explanations* (Minneapolis: University of Minnesota Press, 1980).

Woodward, C. Vann. *The Burden of Southern History* (Baton Rouge: Louisiana State University Press, 1960).

Yeats, W. B. *The Collected Poems of W. B. Yeats* (New York: MacMillan Publishing Co., Inc., 1974).

Farmer Millard Vaughn's shed, formerly a cotton house off the Bellamy Road, 1987.
Photograph © Barbara B. Gibbs. Used by permission.

190

acknowledgments

I have never accomplished anything really important to me without the help
of other people. I am thankful for the friends of this work who buttressed and
sustained it—and me—over a period of nearly twenty years. Without their help,
I wouldn't be writing these words.

The Florida Progress Corporation (known, in 2007 as Progress Energy), led
by Andrew Hines, funded an early and crucial portion of my research, and Florida
Humanities Council audiences across Florida listened patiently to embryonic
portions of the manuscript and asked questions that illuminated the path I was
writing along.

In researching this book, I have been supported by librarians at Santa Fe
Regional Library, Suwannee Valley Regional and Columbia County libraries,
Lake City Community College, and Florida State University's Strozier Library.
At the University of Mississippi, Royce Kurtz and his staff, especially Barbara
Allen, at the J. D. Wiliams Library enthusiastically steered me through the stacks
and dug out old maps. I am also most appreciative to Kenneth W. Johnson for
allowing me access to the site of Santa Fe de Toloca.

I thank many Floridians: first, those I interviewed and theirs families, as well
as Alachuans, Hal Cauthen (who drew the book's contemporary maps), Frank
Cellon, and, most especially, Vada Horner, for their assistance and counsel. The
photography of Barbara B. Gibbs inspired me to undertake this work which, as
it grew, was strengthened by input from readers Bill Cliett, Jenifer Elmore, Ellen
Griffin, Susan Lilley, Meredith Pierce, Nick Wynne, the late Sam Proctor, and
particularly Margaret Langstaff. I am also indebted to Betty Camp, the late El
Cann (former editor of the *High Springs Herald* who, in 1960, sent me out on

my first interviews with area old-timers), Sheridan Bagwell, Sally Graham, Joann Ihas, Will Irby, Joe Knetsch, Pat Nichelson, the late Dan Quinn, Rayford Riels, Sally Rist, Joann Sheppard, Mike Sheppard, Enid Shomer, Nikki Taylor, Allen Tyree, Mary Alice Warren, Larry Westmoreland, and Pam Williamson, for many varieties of moral and practical support. The help of Lee Covell and the late Laura Newman is beyond calculation. I am grateful that writer Bibi Wein, of New York City, advised me during the final review of the manuscript. Many thanks to William A. Hunt for his photographs and to Janet Moses for her drawing. Also much gratitude to Hospice of Central Florida and for the counsel of Bettie McCall.

These unforgettable Mississippians were generous at pivotal moments: Barbara Blansett, who happened along just as I was about to throw out Chapter Nine; John Cook, who has regularly rescued the manuscript from the vagaries of my computers; Vickie Cook and Mike Wright, who allowed me to hunker down in their North Mississippi farmhouse for ten weeks of rewriting; Wil Cook, for believing in this book from 1990 when he was ten years old; Wendy Garrison, for studying Alachua's wildflowers and architecture with me; Arlene Sindelar, for our discussions of Southern religion; Anne and Warren Steel, for so thoroughly praising my rough first draft; and my landlady, the late Opal Miller Worthy, who read every word I wrote while I was in Mississippi. James Tyson's help, an education in itself, was absolutely crucial.

I owe an enormous thank you to my publisher, George F. Thompson, and to his talented editorial staff at the Center for American Places in Staunton, Virginia. Their hard work, patience, and kindness brought this project to completion. Thanks, also, to Dawn Hachenski, for her sensitive book design.

I am not the same person who left Alachua for Mississippi in 1990 and, week after week, climbed the staircase to her mentor's office in the University of Mississippi's Barnard Observatory. Astounded by the encouragement I found at the top of the stairs, I thank Charles Reagan Wilson, for the immense gift of his unwavering belief in the value of my efforts.

Sudye Cauthen was born in Gainesville, Florida, in 1943 and reared in nearby Alachua. She earned a B.A. in English at the University of Central Florida and an M.A. in Southern Studies at the University of Mississippi. She published her first poem at age fourteen and has been documenting North Florida's culture in oral histories, fiction, nonfiction, poetry, videotape, and photography since 1960. She directed Florida's first Folk-Arts-in-the-Schools Program, the Florida Humanities Council's Alachua Portrait Project (for which, in 1984, she received the Tenth Annual Human Rights Award from the Baha' is of Greater Gainesville) and *From the Bellamy Road: Alachua's Beginnings*, a project partially funded by Talquin and the Florida Progress Corporation.

Cauthen has taught writing at the University of Central Florida, Florida State University, North Florida Community College, Lake City Community College, and in other settings, including Poetry-in-the-Schools in Brevard, Orange, and Alachua counties. Her work has appeared in *The Chattahoochee Review*, *The New Encyclopedia of Southern Culture*, *The Florida Review*, *International Quarterly*, *Kalliope*, *The Marjorie Kinnan Rawlings Journal of Florida Literature*, and other journals, newspapers, and magazines. Her writing awards include a State of Florida Individual Artist Fellowship in Literature and a *Glimmer Train* award for Fiction. In 1997, Cauthen founded The North Florida Center for Documentary Studies in White Springs, where she lives and works in a house overlooking Florida's famed Suwannee River.

CENTER FOR
AMERICAN
PLACES

The Center for American Places is a tax-exempt 501(c)(3) nonprofit organization, founded in 1990 by George F. Thompson. Its educational mission is to enhance the public's understanding of, appreciation for, and affection for the places of the Americas and the rest of the world—whether urban, suburban, rural, or wild. Underpinning this mission is the belief that books provide an indispensable foundation for comprehending and caring for the places where we live, work, and explore. Books live. Books endure. Books make a difference Books are gifts to civilization.

With offices in Santa Fe, New Mexico, and Staunton, Virginia, Center editors have brought to publication more than 300 books under the Center's own imprint or in association with numerous publishing partners. Center books have won or shared more than 100 editorial awards and citations, including multiple best book honors in more than thirty academic fields. The Center is also engaged in other outreach programs that emphasize the interpretation of place through exhibitions, lectures, seminars, workshops, and field research. The Center's Cotton Mather Library in Arthur, Nebraska, its Martha A. Strawn Photographic Library in Davidson, North Carolina, and a ten-acre reserve along the Santa Fe River in Florida are available as retreats upon request.

The Center strives every day to make a difference through books, research, and education. For more information, please send inquiries to P.O. Box 23225, Santa Fe, NM 87502, U.S.A., or visit the Center's Website (www.americanplaces.org).

ABOUT THE BOOK:
Southern Comforts: Rooted in a Florida Place was brought to publication in an edition of 2,000 hardcover copies. The text was set in Bernhard Modern and Futura. The paper is Chinese Goldeast Matte Book, 128 gsm weight. The book was printed and bound in China.

FOR THE CENTER FOR AMERICAN PLACES:
George F. Thompson, President and Publisher
Randall B. Jones and Amber K. Lautigar, Associate Editors
Kendall B. McGhee and A. Lenore Lautigar, Editorial Assistants
Kristine K. Harmon and Purna Makaram, Manuscript Editors
Dawn Hachenski, Book Design
David Skolkin, Art Director
David Keck, of Global Ink, Inc., Production Coordinator